EMPOWER *Your* MOMENTUM

Scott Allan is an international bestselling author of over 30 books published in 12 languages in the area of personal growth and self-development. He is the author of *Fail Big*, *Undefeated*, and *Do the Hard Things First*.

As a former corporate business trainer in Japan, and Transformational Mindset Strategist, Scott has invested over 10,000 hours of research and instructional coaching into the areas of self-mastery and leadership training.

With an unrelenting passion for teaching, building critical life skills, and inspiring people around the world to take charge of their lives, Scott Allan is committed to a path of constant and never-ending self-improvement.

Many of the success strategies and self-empowerment material that is reinventing lives around the world evolves from Scott Allan's 20 years of practice and teaching critical skills to corporate executives, individuals, and business owners.

You can connect with Scott at:
scottallan@scottallanpublishing.com
www.scottallanpublishing.com
www.scottallanbooks.com

More Bestselling Titles From Scott Allan

Empower Your Thoughts

Drive Your Destiny

Relaunch Your Life

The Discipline of Masters

Do the Hard Things First

Undefeated

No Punches Pulled

Fail Big

Rejection Free

Built for Stealth

Check out the complete collection of books and training here:
www.scottallanbooks.com

EMPOWER *Your* MOMENTUM

Develop a **Rapid Action Mindset** to **Streamline** Your **Potential** and Get **Massive Results**

SCOTT ALLAN

RUPA

Published by
Rupa Publications India Pvt. Ltd 2025
7/16, Ansari Road, Daryaganj
New Delhi 110002

Sales centres:
Bengaluru Chennai
Hyderabad Jaipur Kathmandu
Kolkata Mumbai Prayagraj

Copyright © Scott Allan 2025

All rights reserved.
No part of this publication may be reproduced, transmitted,
or stored in a retrieval system, in any form or by any means, electronic,
mechanical, photocopying, recording or otherwise, without the prior
permission of the publisher.

P-ISBN: 978-93-5702-749-6
E-ISBN: 978-93-5702-895-0

First impression 2025

10 9 8 7 6 5 4 3 2 1

The moral right of the author has been asserted.

Printed in India

This book is sold subject to the condition that it shall not, by way of
trade or otherwise, be lent, resold, hired out, or otherwise circulated,
without the publisher's prior consent, in any form of binding or
cover other than that in which it is published.

"When you create a vision of the person you most want to become, you begin to build a new identity, and in this journey of creating your confidence, sense of self-worth, and ability to handle life's challenges are limitless."

—Scott Allan

CONTENTS

Introduction   ix

1. Obstacles That Prevent Rapid Action   2
2. Eliminate Self-Defeating Excuses   12
3. The Six Habits for Fueling Determination   22
4. How to Build Massive Momentum   42
5. Take Massive Action on Your Goals   52
6. Setting the Stage for Massive Action   61
7. Developing the Action Mindset   72
8. Create a Strong Sense of Urgency   88
9. How to Prevent Burnout & Never Give Up   100

Conclusion: Take the Five-Day Massive Action Challenge   109

"To stay present in everyday life, it helps to be deeply rooted within yourself; otherwise, the mind, which has incredible momentum, will drag you along like a wild river."

—Eckhart Tolle

INTRODUCTION

ACTION IS THE KEY TO YOUR SUCCESS

Think of the name of any successful person who inspires you, and you'll see that success comes from action. The most successful people in business (and beyond) are all people who took action. We are often specialists in putting off any substantial effort. Once you have clarity on what you want to create, why you want it, and the direction you must go, it's time to turn things up a notch and take massive and immediate action.

That is what this book is about.

So, we want to study, learn, and prepare everything as best as we can before we set out to create our dream business. But by thinking this way, you risk never getting started. You begin to realize the skills you lack and the knowledge you still need to acquire, and you keep putting it off.

Action is the key to your success because it allows you to gain experience, it allows you to fail and this is data you can use to improve, and you can eventually become an expert by trying again with a different approach.

What happens is, out of fear of making a wrong impression, looking dumb, making a bad decision or risking the fragile vulnerability of ego, many people get stuck planning actions instead of taking them.

The key is to **plan and execute**. Through execution, you learn what works and, where on the journey you must refine your skill. You must have clarity on the direction you are moving in, yet avoid getting caught up in making a "perfect plan" before taking action.

Yet, even if it's counterintuitive, the best thing to do is take intentional action as soon as possible. This is also known as deliberate practice, when you are taking deliberate action with the intention of achieving a specific goal. After all, if you dive in blindly and start hacking away at random tasks without adhering to a target, your aim will always miss. You will create negative momentum pulling you in the wrong direction.

The benefit to your project is worth more than the embarrassment of your tentative first steps. Think of Thomas Edison, for example. Before he invented the light bulb, he tried it thousands of times without success. But he never got discouraged. He used the experience of repetitive failing as a data rich stream of information that said, "This doesn't work. Let's try another approach." And so he did, investing in over 10,000 attempts. But the point is, he knew what he wanted to achieve with his actions. Every failure was a stepping stone in building momentum towards the ultimate goal.

The key is to **push forward with relentless consistency**. Winners—successful high-performance entrepreneurs, inventors and creators—tap into this formula and keep trying, over and over again. The people who give up end up losing because they think momentum is all about achieving a successful outcome one after the other. They end up consistently procrastinating and experience a decline in momentum energy.

When you consistently put something off, the price you pay is a guaranteed failure. If you don't start acting today, you'll be in the same situation next year. And the year after that. And eventually a decade will go by and you'll realize that while you were busy procrastinating, somebody else was busy hustling and putting in the work.

Today, you put it off because you need to perfect some part of the plan, but tomorrow, you'll find another reason to do nothing. My best advice for this act of self-sabotage is, don't do this. Throwing yourself into doing something for the first time and failing is not a failure, but instead, it is the fastest way to improve. The good news is that, inaction isn't just unique to you, it is a common evil. Therefore, this gives you an advantage if you act without wasting time.

When you come up with some good ideas, put them into action as soon as possible. Thoughts are often fleeting. If you wait too long, the picture becomes increasingly nebulous, and in the end, you will do nothing with it.

When you do something for the first time, it isn't going to work out. Expect to fail and get used to embarrassing yourself. It is all about learning and gradual improvement. This is true at all stages of your journey.

Action is the key to all your progress, so it's only after the third, tenth, or one-hundredth attempt, that things start to click, and you are playing for real. You have skin in the game. You are creating momentum through trial and error. This is where perseverance kicks in. You will then realize, that "motivation" thing people are always talking about is the result of doing something first, getting a result, and trying again with a slight tweak for improvement.

The faster you implement, the quicker you get through the training phase. There's no such thing as perfection—if you wait until you're perfect, you'll never get going. So, here's where you're better off focusing on constant improvement rather than perfection. And if what you do is 20% okay, that's fine.

It's about always continuing to find a better way, maybe just one small step at a time. There is no end to the possibility of improvement.

Getting started—and taking the first steps—is the most challenging thing. You have to overcome the inertia that holds you back under the guise of needing to plan better or acquire more skills. Initially, overcoming this mental barrier becomes easier as you learn. You will be unstoppable if you combine your actions with progressive time management. We will discuss later at a deeper level in this book.

So, what is stopping you now from actually starting with your business idea? And how can you remove this obstacle? What would allow you to act quickly, knowing that the real game begins after a lot of practice runs? How many times must you practice? There is no magic number. The only words that come to mind are "act now" without hesitation. Don't wait for permission, but rather, give yourself space to just be yourself and dive straight into the work.

If you want to answer these questions and learn the value of taking action to achieve a goal, continue reading. This book teaches learners, business builders, entrepreneurs, and anybody with a desire to WIN, how to take immediate massive action when confronted with the fear of failure, rejection, and analysis paralysis.

The time for building momentum is now.

When you are ready to take the plunge and step into designing greatness, push forward into the first chapter.

There is **no time to waste**.

> *"Excitement must lead to immediate action or you will lose the power of momentum. More dreams die because we fail to seize the moment. Do it now!"*
>
> —Tony Robbins

1
OBSTACLES THAT PREVENT RAPID ACTION

Before we dive into and break down the limiting beliefs and thoughts that prevent you from taking action, let's look at the nature of obstacles and what they mean. Obstacles—roadblocks, problems, or challenges—are inevitable, and you can't ignore things stopping you from moving forward. The question is, "What will you do about it?"

A life without obstacles is a life without progress. If you're not growing, you're dying. You are here to solve problems and bust through life's difficulties to elevate yourself to the next best level. You build the foundation for long-term momentum when you do this and take definitive action toward your goals.

Necessity drives us to do what we were born to—find solutions to life's challenges through creativity, perseverance, and resilience.

Every question expects an answer, and every doubt requires clarification. The mind (when used correctly) serves precisely this purpose, to overcome the obstacles that present themselves to transform us into whomever we choose to be.

The mind is a creative engine. Every thought formed tends to manifest itself in its corresponding physical experience, whether you choose to visualize the future you desire and identify with it or get emotionally involved with the gruesome images on the news. Today's internal emotion and focus generate tomorrow's external experience.

A goal that does not present difficulties to be overcome is not a worthy goal, and a victory without a battle is not an actual win. Do you want to see the other side of success after many years of struggling? Push through the darkness. Do you want to reach your goal? You must face the obstacles that separate you from them.

Momentum is built within by doing the things that cause you discomfort.

Difficulty creates necessity, forcing you to innovate and evolve into a better version of yourself. Conditions make demands, and demands create action, leading to results. The evolutionary process is constantly at work, building your future from the present moment you live.

If you had not encountered obstacles, you would not be as you are now. Every obstacle you overcame yesterday allowed you to become who you are today.

Through his experiments on plant parasites, **Jacques Lock**, a member of the Rockefeller Institute, demonstrated how even the smallest beings adapt to the natural change that life imposes and through which it thrives and spreads.

J. Lock placed pots with roses in front of windows. As long as it was alive, the aphids of the plant drew nourishment from its sap. These aphids had no wings. But the rose, purposely left without water, died after a few days. The aphids encountered an obstacle—they had lost their nourishment. These little creatures then grew temporary wings to fly away toward the window's light.

Nature is the perfect example of survival. It will find a way to live, and anything that doesn't find a way becomes extinct. If there are limits to what you think you can achieve, they are created by your mind, but this doesn't mean your limitations are real. Limits are but illusions that we believe to be real. Momentum results from what you think and believe you can achieve. When you push hard to break the barriers of your excuses and the comforts of laziness, you develop a mind and body built to withstand hard times. Momentum is a force that will push you through the toughest of circumstances.

The solution to your opposing challenge is revealed when you focus on the goal. Ask yourself, "How do I get from here to there? What is blocking me?"

It's a process of continuous refinement.

THE CHALLENGE WITH TAKING ACTION

Now that we understand the nature of transcending obstacles, let's look at the roadblocks preventing you from taking action.

Awareness of the psychological mechanisms that usually turn us away from taking action helps to put your goals into practice. To highlight an example, let's think about business meetings. You may have spent part of the day discussing these with colleagues and managers.

"Another useless meeting… it's just a waste of time," is the expected outcome after being dragged through a two-hour board meeting. Why is it that meetings are useless or hardly bring anything concrete?

After a business meeting or training course, there are often many negative comments about the pain points of running a business. The purpose of these meetings is to propose solutions to improve the organizational or logistical aspects of the company. Often, we are not talking about tackling complex structural problems—which would require a significant commitment, for example, in economic terms—but we are talking about what could be done immediately, concretely, to achieve instant improvement.

We're talking about something other than moving the business abroad or taking over a more prominent company or a store in the city center. We attended the meeting full of enthusiasm to share new ideas and valuable suggestions to change things. What happened after the session? During the meeting, everyone agreed that a good team atmosphere is full of enthusiasm, excitement, and energy for the goals set. Then, we go back to our workplaces as if nothing happened, and everything goes back to how it was before.

Why is it so difficult to practice what was established in the meeting? What happens to the "plan" that everyone was so enthusiastic about? Months later, those who attended the meeting find themselves saying:

- "Everything stayed the same, you know. Besides, time being what it is, there's always so much to do…"
- "Yes, the meeting was exciting, but when I get to the company, there are a thousand things to do; time flies… I can no longer make up my mind or track time."
- "For goodness sake! Better not to question what's working, just in case…."
- "Changing things is always difficult. Employees have their habits, you know…."
- "But this is how we've always done things, so why change now?"

And so, everything remains the same as before—very few implement concrete changes, and most ideas born during the meeting remain pure theory. Why is it that good intentions don't always become a reality?

BETWEEN SAYING AND DOING, THERE IS THE MIDDLE "GIVE"

We must get used to commitment, decisions, leadership, confidence, energy, work, creativity, concreteness, and actions. In other words, provide "facts." Concreteness that's what we lack. You should, before complaining and criticizing, examine your intentions and ask yourself:

- "What have I done concretely?"
- "What have I given?"
- "Have I committed the best of myself and energy?"
- "Did I put my full effort into making positive change?"

The difference between "talking" and "doing" is simply asking whether you are doing everything you can to shift momentum. Remember this: **momentum is created from the inertia of action fueled by the intent to achieve a better outcome.**

It is the basis of self-realization—the knowledge that you have done something and attempted to change the course of events. This makes us feel good and creates that sense of fulfillment we all desire. To arrive home at night, look back on the day, and see the result of an achievement that was only possible because you did something about it.

"IT CAN'T BE DONE"

If our ancestors who first appeared on Earth had thought this way, we probably wouldn't be here. Let's not just use our "inability to act" as an excuse not to do things or face problems. Let's not limit ourselves to paying for other people's time with money; let's not let others decide our activity. It's too easy to sit back and complain that things aren't going well because you're not "getting it." Don't take the easy way and sit back, watching others achieve greatness when you can also be great.

To truly change reality, we must take actions we have never taken before and become the kind of person we have always wanted to be. We will always get the same results if we continue to act as we always have.

From now on, be aware of these negative phrases that keep you stuck:

- "Nothing changes anyway."
- "That's just the way I am."
- "Nothing ever works out for me, so why bother."
- "I'll wait until somebody else does it first, and then I'll consider it."

These are certainly not the best phrases for achieving momentum. Momentum, by the way, does not always mean a spiral upsurge. Taking action without a strategy can lead to a counterintuitive result.

Real change requires radical innovation. If you're not ready to engage, you're faking it.

Today, we are all attracted to instant success. We have all heard legends about the guy who picked up a pin from the ground and is now a millionaire, about the person who was in the right place at the right time and is now the CEO of that company. How a young entrepreneur founded an app and sold it for billions

We are influenced by the media and collective thinking that proposes easy success in the face of poor quality. This is the American dream—a fortune that comes too quickly and easily for everyone. Brilliant minds, in reality, are sporadic, and they don't necessarily lead to success. We all have the same intellectual and practical resources—the difference lies in the individual's mindset, tenacity, ferocity, will, and ability to take action and persevere through difficult times.

There is never any guarantee of success; the only guarantee is that it will be difficult.

Those who have succeeded are not superhuman, but people like us. Their days lasted 24 hours, had lots of good ideas (and not-so-good ones), and they worked through many difficult times. But they kept "doing" and "trying" and "improvising" to solve problems and overcome difficulties.

Momentum is built through failure.

Everyone makes mistakes, but absolute failure is failing to get back up after making those mistakes. How many of us, to change our lives, play the lottery? How many people have already decided how to spend the winnings?

Dreaming is excellent, but only if you act toward your dreams. Instead of envying those who have been successful, use it as an opportunity to say, "I can do it, too!" The first step to "do" is to be aware that you have to engage your time and energy. First, we must do it for ourselves, and then we can teach others how to do it. Only those genuinely fulfilled within themselves can find the energy to devote to helping others.

Let's start moving forward. What's the next step? This, too, is communication—it tells others we feel like doing (or not doing) something. If we get used to tackling the simplest activities right away, we will discover how easy it is to put the most complex projects into action. It's about taking small steps forward and racking up small wins. This is called progress, and progress builds momentum.

"Doing" is not that difficult! After all, even the highest peak is reached one step at a time.

FEAR OF CHANGE

Change is difficult—leaving our usual "comfort zone" to venture into an unknown place. Change gives us the power to modify our habits to touch our deepest emotional and psychological levers.

We will not dwell on all aspects of change but evaluate its effects in practice. When we choose to make a change, it is usually more reassuring to replicate the actions and behaviors already experienced. For example:

- If we meet people at a party, we will likely approach those we already know first.
- If we need to make a purchase, we first go to a store we have bought from before.
- If we have to go across town to a new place, we usually walk down familiar streets.

Often, going down the road (in a broad sense) already traveled—repeating choices similar to those made previously—is simply a form of mental "laziness." We naturally want to commit little, spend little, and risk as little as possible. In other words, to save our resources and energy for fear of a future emergency.

Maintaining the same habits requires no effort; it doesn't cost us energy or willpower and doesn't disturb our state of intimate stillness or comfort. On the contrary, change requires commitment and courage, generates anxiety, and challenges our mental laziness. You will experience this when you try to push outside your comfort zone.

The good news is that action is habit-forming. The first few times, we will struggle, but then, with consistent and deliberate practice and the experience of succeeding in something new, acting without hesitation will come naturally. But even when you fail, this information is vital in helping you to change your course.

TO CONCLUDE

The time for excuses and justifications is over. Everyone talks, procrastinates, and makes excuses for not doing something, especially those without specific experience, telling others what they should do.

It's time to take action without expecting extraordinary things. Let's aim for activities that we can do and are within our reach that will truly bring change. Let us all examine our conscience and evaluate our capacity to take action.

The question we need to ask ourselves is:

"Are we ready to give rather than receive, to get everything done?

"Success is not the key to happiness. Happiness is the key to success. If you love what you are doing, you will be successful."

—Albert Schweitzer

2
ELIMINATE SELF-DEFEATING EXCUSES

This chapter will cover the ten most common excuses that pull us away from our goals. Moreover, we will look at the positive thoughts that will neutralize the negative impact of the excuses and drive you to take immediate action when the time calls for it.

There was a period in history when we experienced demographic, economic, and cultural deterioration… no, I'm not talking about the present day. I'm talking about the dark ages, the Middle Ages. The Roman Empire collapsed, and the entire world at that time sank into a deep nightmare. But do you know what happened at the end of this dark period? Many people relied on the light they had burning inside, and that's how the Renaissance began.

This historical period radically changed the paradigms of the human being and saw the flourishing of artistic and cultural disciplines, especially in Italy, the cradle of this evolution of consciousness. This rebirth led human beings to view the world and themselves differently. The Renaissance began because darkness allowed light to spread.

Obstacles serve to improve your life and not hinder it. Even if everything seems wrong, remember that spring always follows winter. If you like rainbows, you must accept the rain; if you want to see the stars, embrace the night; if you're going to admire the rise of a new dawn, cross the darkness with your purpose in mind.

For this reason, we must not allow excuses to impede our progress. We must not hold ourselves back from taking action out of fear or uncertainty.

"I'll do it tomorrow," "I don't have time," "I'm not good at it"… you've likely uttered all of these phrases a few times and built a wall between you and your goals. Goals are the engine of our lives. However, because of fear, uncertainty, lack of self-confidence, or the unknown, we end up running away from the idea of dreaming, imagining, or planning.

This is when excuses start to appear. They are not the same for everyone, as each person is a world unto themselves, but they all sound the same. It doesn't matter what your goal is, how difficult it is to achieve, or what needs to be done to make it come true. Putting aside your excuses and focusing on achieving your goals is vital.

EXCUSE #1: "I'M TOO OLD NOW"

I hear this phrase far too often. It's not our age but how old we feel. During one of my trips to Australia, while Couchsurfing with my friend Sam, I met Jackie, her mom. White-haired, strong-willed, at the age of 70, she packed her backpack, said goodbye to everyone, and set off to tour Europe… solo, of course! And there are many people like her. Let's not limit ourselves.

This excuse turns into: "I permit myself to embark on new adventures."

EXCUSE #2: "IT'S NEVER WORKED FOR ME"

With this excuse, it's like telling ourselves there's no point in trying because it won't work. We foreshadow a failure scenario that justifies us from not taking the first step.

Nothing will indeed change, and it might even be that you'll go from one disaster into another, but how do you know if you don't try and give up before you even start?

It's a matter of accepting that you can't have any certainties and that no matter how well you predict the consequences and outcomes of your actions, there will always be the unexpected to surprise you. But do you want to feel the satisfaction of taking charge of your life and trying?

This excuse turns into: "I am aware that past failures will not affect my future if I don't allow them to."

EXCUSE #3: "I'M NOT READY YET"

We will always need more time to feel ready to do anything. How many more classes will we have to take to feel prepared? And how many times will we have to revise our project before we deliver it to the client?

The only solution to this excuse is to get started! Do it when you are 60% ready, without waiting until you are 100% ready! There are no excuses! To get where you want, you must take the first step, then the second, and follow all the others. But if you don't start, you'll never get there!

So begin. Take one small step—the first action. Do the easy thing first but do something.

This excuse turns into perfectionism, which is the enemy of proficiency; now, I have started and will gradually improve as I go along.

EXCUSE #4: "I'M TOO BUSY RIGHT NOW"

The quintessential phrase of the 21st century. We always move at a thousand miles an hour and only have a minute for the essential things. Our days go by, and ultimately, we don't enjoy anything. The current pace of life is hectic, no one can deny that, but it is also true that wanting is power. Don't hide behind the excuse of not having free time to do things.

Doing what we need to do is a matter of priority. If there were something you were passionate about, you'd find a few free minutes, wake up earlier, take a faster mode of transportation, not work overtime, etc. Analyze how you spend your time before using it as an excuse.

We all have 24 hours a day, but managing our time makes the difference. It's not about time, and it's about priorities.

Want to read 52 books in a year? Check how much time you spend on social media or surfing the web. Read the book on your lunch break, turn off the TV, and start with a few pages at night before bed.

This excuse turns into: "I learned to manage my time well."

EXCUSE #5: "I'M NO GOOD AT THAT"

When pursuing our dreams or making a tough decision, we can feel a lack of self-confidence, convincing us that we'll never make it. If we let it, this little voice could become paralyzing, leading to inaction and inertia.

The antidote to this excuse is to learn to recognize that you are doing your best and will continue to do your best to make things work no matter what. Let yourself make mistakes, not get everything right the first time, and get there in stages. Remove the "not" and "never" from your thoughts and replace them with the sentence below.

This excuse turns into: "I'm going to make it my way and at a time that works for me."

Excuse #6: "I can do it next week."

According to this excuse, our choices must follow a linear and equal direction in which each step prepares us for the next.

In reality, our life takes us from point A to point Z along a path that is anything but straight. It is full of curves, detours, and the unexpected. And often, this means that change is just around the corner; it happens when you least expect it or make a decision you hadn't planned for as you thought the conditions were right the day before.

The conditions will always be challenging, and this is the only truth.

If you wait until all the conditions are in place, you're expecting to be 100% ready before you act, and in most cases, everything is the same. The more you put something off, the less likely you will commit to finishing it.

Next week turns into next month, and this transitions into next year. I can name several projects that I have put off for years. But it begins with the phrase, "I can do it later."

Don't plan to do it tomorrow if you can do it right now.

This excuse turns into: "The only certainty I have is here and now; I act in the present despite condemning it to uncertainty."

EXCUSE #7: "NOW IS NOT THE TIME"

There is no such thing as the right or wrong time.

Sometimes, it's just that we're still getting ready for a radical step, and we need a little more time to transform our fears.

This excuse turns into: "What would I do if I wasn't afraid?"

EXCUSE #8: "MY (SPOUSE/PARENTS/FRIENDS) THINK IT'S A BAD IDEA"

"What will others think?" The "what will they say" mentality has always worried us, and we must accept it. What will my parents think if I drop out of school because I don't like this faculty? What will my wife say if I give up my job to pursue a passion of mine? How will my friends react if I tell them I have decided to start my own business?

You can't control the opinions or thoughts of others. You can listen to their advice and consider the suggestions they're making. They will always have reasons to criticize your choices, no matter what you do. If you care what others say about your actions, talk to your loved ones before making a decision, but ensure you always have the final say.

You will never be in a position where you can please everybody; the only thing that matters is how you feel about yourself. If you're OK with it, Roll the dice and start moving.

This excuse turns into: "I am aware of and responsible for my choices; I am my boss."

EXCUSE #9: "I DON'T HAVE THE MONEY"

A lack of money is an objective fact that you must accept. However, we often give ourselves this excuse without verifying our genuine willingness to invest in a change or perhaps convincing ourselves that changing things will require money beyond our reach. If we delve deeper, we may discover this is different.

Knowing your natural financial resources and planning your income and expenses is as important as having an accurate prospectus of how much money you should spend to make the change you want, whether quitting your job and starting your own business or moving house. The amount is quite different from what you had imagined (for better or worse), and being aware of your actual situation can also clarify your motivations. But if you don't have a clear idea of the "numbers" first, you will hardly be able to understand if the excuse you are telling yourself is legitimate or dictated by fear.

And it is important to be honest with yourself and recognize your priorities. Are you sure that you need that bag or that you can't limit yourself to just one drink a week to put something aside and finally be able to afford that course you've been putting off for a while?

This excuse turns into: "I am aware of my economy and choose wisely how to use it for my personal growth."

EXCUSE #10: "I'LL LOOK STUPID AS USUAL"

Lack of self-esteem is a serious problem that does not allow us to make our dreams come true. We can move forward and achieve our goals if we have confidence in our abilities. No one is born knowing things—don't forget that. You may need more experience, knowledge, or practice, but never say that you are "good-for-nothing," even when things don't go as you would like.

Behind this excuse is the fear of change, which is very often considered a selfish gesture. That is because, to change, we need to listen to ourselves, put ourselves and our needs at the center, change the state of things, and understand the repercussions on those around us, not just on us.

In addition, we are not used to distinguishing goals that are good for us from what we think is expected of us (or from goals that seem right according to "common sense"). So we hardly listen to ourselves, and when we think of making a change in our lives, we are assailed by doubts and fear of being ridiculed.

This excuse turns into: "I accept that I won't be able to be at everyone's beck and call and that mockery defines the giver, not the receiver."

These excuses take us away from our goals, and it doesn't matter if it's to change jobs, get in shape, or learn a new language—they are there lurking, ready to turn off enthusiasm, goodwill, and motivation with immediate effect!

They are the excuses we make to tell ourselves that it's not worth it and that, at the moment, we are not willing to change our habits and put ourselves on the line for something that we don't know will improve our current condition. We justify ourselves because we are unwilling to pay the price of change and leave the certain for the uncertain. And this happens even if the "certain" is a little tight and uncomfortable for us... even if we start asking questions and wondering what it's like "on the other side" of the barricade of our comfort zone.

And as we tell ourselves about it, the situation in which we find ourselves already seems more acceptable, we almost come to like it, and our comfort zone no longer looks so wrong. So much so that we doubt why we ever wanted to change.

In our comfort zone, the subtle discomfort we feel is known to us, and while it is true that, on the one hand, we do not experience the thrill of novelty, on the other hand, we shelter ourselves from risk, failure, and worry about the unknown. Nothing happens there, yet that's where we prefer to be when we want to feel in control of the situation.

And when we become accustomed to tolerating the background noise by ensuring a good level of tranquility and security, our brains try to protect us from possible risks that leaving our comfort zone might entail. This is how we activate a long list of excuses that shelter us from the "danger of novelty." And the more we fear change, the more we talk ourselves out of taking action.

*"A year from now you'll wish
you had started today."*

—Karen Lamb

3

THE SIX HABITS FOR FUELING DETERMINATION

I often hear about people's daily problems—obstacles, delays, separations, rejections, failures, and deteriorating physical or mental conditions. Yet, many people who undergo life's challenges persevere, overcome significant challenges, and lead successful lives. What does success mean, and how do people achieve it? What internal characteristics do these individuals possess, and what external factors have been present in their lives? What strengths do we need to invest in to overcome our challenges?

Determination combines skills, knowledge, and beliefs that enable a person to commit to goals, self-regulating through autonomous behavior. Understanding one's strengths and limitations, coupled with extreme self-confidence, is essential to one's determination. When acting on these skills and attitudes, individuals have a more extraordinary ability to take control of their lives and become successful adults.

Gaining control over your life involves knowledge, applying goal setting to achieve in the work, sports, or personal spheres, understanding your abilities and limitations, and developing problem-solving and self-analysis. The unique learning process, using self-assessment of your skills and awareness, is at the heart of finding the determination to achieve your success. This chapter will discuss the role of determination and willpower in taking massive action and getting results.

DO ONE THING AT A TIME WITH YOUR FULL ATTENTION

Have you ever been tempted, even a little, by the myth of multitasking? That is the idea that managing multiple things simultaneously is beneficial to productivity.

As a good introvert, I've always preferred concentrating on one thing at a time simultaneously. But for a few years now, I've been working in a chaotic office full of stimuli, where I often bounce from one activity to another like a pinball.

It has taken me a long time to realize that this is one of the causes of my work stress. It is clear that multitasking is not for me and that to learn to work better, I will need to use strategies to keep my attention focused on one task at a time and learn to manage interruptions and pressures.

Yet this myth of multitasking exists. Many people are convinced that frantically switching between tasks and dividing their attention across multiple fronts is a great way to be more productive. Doing one thing at a time (perhaps with care and attention) is no longer in vogue and almost seems like a waste of time. But is that the case?

Let's clarify one thing—multitasking does not exist. The brain is not capable of devoting attention to several activities at the same time. When we have the sensation of doing several things at once, in truth, we do nothing but shift our attention from one activity to another very quickly.

Office work often goes like this... you open a file, write three lines, then a phone call comes in, and you must go out and find some documents. After the phone call, you look at your emails, and finally, an answer has arrived for a job you left undone.

So, you open another file to complete the pending stuff,

but when you're about to finish, a colleague comes to ask you something important. Then you go back to your computer, have two files open, and you have to remember which one you were working on. You magically put in 15 minutes of work, during which you half-finish the thing and resume your initial file, but at that moment, the boss calls you. You grab a pen and paper and rush into his office, only to come out with a new urgent task to do. In the meantime, your cell phone rings, more emails arrive, and you need to call the mechanic to have your car serviced... and so on, until the end of the day.

To some, this is an excellent way to work. It is the thought that so many tasks, so many tools, so much technology, and so much speed also bring excellent efficiency and productivity. But someone in recent years has put forward some doubt, saying that multitasking is, in truth, nonsense. It doesn't make us more productive but more stressed, and maybe it's even worse for the brain.

Stanford University conducted one of the first research in this direction in 2009. Others have followed to confirm that multitasking doesn't work. Here's why:

- It's not true that it increases productivity. It's just the opposite. Moving from one task to another always requires adjustment time. Every time we change jobs, our brain has to pick up somehow the thread of what it was doing, which takes time and energy. So, constantly bouncing from one task to another waste our time. It's more efficient to do one job at a time, finish it, and move on to the next.
- It increases errors. Attention is a scarce resource. Quickly alternating between different tasks, working in bits and pieces on this, and keeping an eye on emails and open chats strains our attention span and concentration. We

work more superficially and make more mistakes.
- It is stressful and, in the long run, increases the risk of anxiety, depression, attention disorders, and hyperactivity problems.
- It harms relationships with people. Giving others partial and fragmented attention while thinking about your work, answering a text message, or checking Facebook is unsuitable for relationships, whether with colleagues, family, or friends.

So, we've made it clear that multitasking is stressful, it kills our productivity, yet it's hard to do without it. Sometimes it's because the work environment pushes us towards this wrong way of working. Sometimes it's because we're hunting for stimuli to lighten up mentally demanding tasks. But how can we eliminate this toxic and unproductive habit to work better, get more results, and feel less stressed? Here are a few tips:

- **Go on a social media diet. Start cutting your time on** social media, messaging, blogging, and online information. Get into the habit of doing one thing at a time. Keep your smartphone away while you study, or at least turn off the notifications. Don't keep your tablet handy if you decide to watch some TV.
- **Use the "Pomodoro Technique" to organize your study or work time.** Stay focused on what you need to do for 25 minutes, then take a five-minute break. Working or studying using this technique helps you not bounce from one task to another like a crazy ball and slowly trains your ability to stay focused on one task at a time.
- **Reason by priority.** If your to-do list has become too long, stop and think for a moment. When everything seems urgent

and essential, everything looks the same. We are active and busy, but that doesn't necessarily mean we are also productive. So, try not to fall into this trap. Scroll through your to-do list and highlight two to three essential things. Meanwhile, do those and try not to give in to the pressure of everything else.

- **Manage interruptions.** You can't say yes to everyone. If you've identified your current priority and are trying to focus, you can only give in to some who ask for your attention. Evaluate the request and if you decide it's not urgent or a priority, explain to the interrupter that you can't take care of their problem at that time. Make a note immediately, and then remember to contact the person as soon as you're available. Giving others 100% of our attention whenever possible is always better.

- **And finally, meditate.** While researching this article, I couldn't help but notice that multitasking is the exact opposite of mindfulness. Suppose mindfulness means being absorbed in the present, aware of body and mind together. In that case, multitasking looks like its opposite—that *monkey mind* brings us so much anxiety and confusion.

Professor David Levy, an information technology expert at the University of Washington, and a group of researchers experimented to understand if meditating affected multitasking. A group of people was asked to simulate a typical office situation—each had to set the date of a meeting, agree on it with other participants, look for a free room, and write a brief presentation of the forum and a draft program. They had little time to complete their work. The information needed to accomplish the assigned tasks arrived by email, phone, messaging systems, and directly from people knocking on the door.

After the simulation, the researchers divided the participants into several groups. One of these groups took a meditation course for eight weeks. In the end, all participants—those who had taken the meditation course and those who had not—repeated the simulation. What emerged?

Those who had done meditation for eight weeks perceived a lower stress level in performing tasks. In addition, the group of those who had meditated organized their work differently, lingering longer on each duty, and making fewer transitions from one activity to another, but without lengthening the overall time to complete the job. In practice, those who had learned to meditate had also known not to react immediately to interruptions at work, keeping their attention focused.

The research did not find that those who had meditated also increased productivity or improved accuracy in carrying out tasks. However, the group of those who had meditated did remember the details of the work more accurately.

What are you waiting for? Implement these tips into your life, and your stress levels will drop dramatically. Please don't get caught up in wanting to do it all. Remember to start with one tiny step at a time. You can introduce one strategy and gradually integrate it with the others. Note that even if you develop only one of the techniques shown, the improvement will be huge!

WHEN FEAR IS BLOCKING YOU, DO THAT THING YOU'RE AFRAID OF.

Moments of difficulty, failure, and loss occur in our lives. No matter how hard we try, these circumstances are often unavoidable. When faced with these situations, people fall into two broad categories—those who succumb, pick themselves up, and get going again. Both are afraid of not making it, but when faced with it, they react very differently. How can we transform ourselves from people who think they won't make it—and therefore fail—to men and women who can positively react to adversity and challenges?

What makes the difference are the experiences we have had in life and the way we react to them. A series of failures can play a role in our children's experiences, particularly our parents' parenting style. Having been told often, "You'll never make it," or "I'm sure you will," can make a massive difference in a person's future.

But the good news is that we continue to learn, and the brain continues to adapt even in adult life; therefore, we can reverse course by improving our ability to respond to events. The latest research in neuroplasticity confirms that the brain learns continuously, and if we can pilot our experiences and change our habits, we will transform our inner reality.

Who wouldn't want to live to the fullest, to enjoy this wonderful gift that is life? We can all do it, even if we learn to manage our emotional reactions to the best of our ability. We all live with emotions and what we can achieve by learning to manage them is not the illusion of avoiding problems, but the certainty of knowing how to deal with them, to be able to react and use them as opportunities for learning and growth.

A matter of self-esteem: Faced with a problem or a challenge, the first action we all take at an unconscious level is to analyze whether we have the resources to deal with it successfully or not. Suppose this analysis results in a negative response, the fear of not succeeding turns into a block for our eventual actions and reactions.

Therefore, it is not the type of problem we are facing that makes the difference, but our level of self-esteem, how much we believe in ourselves, how much confidence we have in ourselves, or—on the contrary—how little we believe in our abilities.

Good levels of self-esteem translate into a perception of ability in the face of the problem and encourage positive action. On the other hand, low self-esteem means perceiving scarce resources that tend to succumb passively in the face of difficulty. This is why people tend to be either able or unable to overcome challenges, regardless of the type of problem they face.

There is, however, an excellent margin for improvement starting from the analysis of one's strengths and weaknesses, which usually occurs quickly and unconsciously, and that can instead be made more rational and objective. I often use the SWOT analysis—a table widely used in the business world—to identify our strengths, weaknesses, opportunities, and threats. In this way, it becomes much clearer that, in any situation, we have resources we can trust.

Acquiring more objectivity concerning ourselves also allows us to ignore that hypercritical side that tends towards perfectionism. After all, our society and the educational system create standardized approaches to problems, and anything that doesn't work according to a specific standard is considered abnormal.

This invites people to adhere to a particular pattern of action or behavior and be implicitly hypercritical when they don't fit it. However, the expected behavior is only sometimes the best fit for us as individuals in the face of our specific problems.

Therefore, we must develop the courage not to self-censor our creativity in the face of difficulty. Fear of making mistakes and failure is undoubtedly one of the main mechanisms of self-sabotage in work, affection, and achieving new perspectives.

But fear is there to teach us how best to act, not to block us. This is why fear is a natural feeling and has accompanied you at every stage of the journey. If you look at fear as a brake, it represents a natural trap of your mind destined to prevent us from living fully.

If, on the contrary, you look at it as an opportunity to improve yourself, you'll get out of the trap, and you'll start to see the world and challenges from a different perspective. Living fully and experiencing the pleasure of success means not being afraid of making mistakes but finding the resources to face obstacles head-on.

We are coming out of loneliness to overcome the crisis. The person with low self-esteem fails to live fully and address the issues that arise before him and isolates himself from others in the belief that he has something wrong that must be hidden.

Often, this leads to feelings of loneliness, marginalization, frustration, and natural depression that harm health. Today, we know that the quality of our relationships determines our lives and, in many ways, our health.

Isolation often leads to insomnia, anxiety, and mood decline, which, in turn, encourages the search for compensation stimuli such as food, alcohol, or smoking. The person is at risk of entering a downward spiral that dramatically increases stress levels. Because stress is a prevalent disease, people pretend it is not there.

Yet, clinically, stress is something authentic that you can measure with biochemical values (such as salivary sampling of cortisol) or functional (such as the analysis of heart rate variability or HRV). Stress is related to many diseases and should not be overlooked.

Becoming more objective and detached from oneself allows one to discover resources and abilities that remain in the shadows, buried by our insecurities. In this way, self-esteem improves, and this, in turn, gives us the courage we need to act.

Our actions will reward us and thus create a virtuous cycle of increased self-confidence. This has a long list of benefits, starting with a reduced perception of stress and an increased sense of control over one's life.

Seek external encouragement. Once you start on a self-esteem-building journey, you begin to come out of isolation, putting your relationships with the people around you back into play. However, there are dangers in this phase that we need to pay attention to. We must avoid creating forms of dependence on others, and above all, we must not fall into the trap of constantly seeking the approval of others.

Living fully means living our lives and not denying our own needs to try to meet the needs of others. There are profound reciprocal influences between people who hang out in a positive and hostile environment. The research speaks of "social contagion" to define how fundamental the people we hang out with are in determining our habits and even our happiness levels.

So, we need to find the courage to break the toxic bonds we know are hurting us and network with people who strengthen our desire to grow and feel good. This is only sometimes accomplished on our own. In this case, professional support can help us gain clarity on how not to be crushed by the judgment of others and how to create a network of healthy and sincere friendships.

Regain motivation with sports. Physical activity plays a fundamental role in overcoming the fear of making mistakes and strengthening self-esteem. Doing sports means putting yourself on the line, accepting a challenge in a predefined context protected by rules that make it easier to overcome your fears.

Physical activity also has an essential effect on the brain because it helps restore the proper relationship between neurotransmitters and promotes neuroplasticity, adapting our brains to new experiences. Movement stimulates BDNF (brain-derived neurotrophic factor), which repairs and regenerates the brain.

The sport also leads to pride and satisfaction and directly benefits self-esteem because you see yourself better and feel more energetic.

When developing a comprehensive training program, I always recommend evaluating at least two kinds of activity—long-term cardiovascular and muscular endurance and strength. This is because endurance and strength are both characteristics of our bodies that must be preserved. The metabolic responses induced by the two forms of training are different and synergistic.

Consider doing circuit training with weights twice a week and brisk walking at least two more times. Both types of workouts can be about 45 minutes long.

Follow an anti-stress diet. The food we choose to eat represents how much we love ourselves. Taking back control of your diet is essential in building higher self-esteem and health.

Proper nutrition involves, first and foremost, a balance of macronutrients. For example, eliminating important protein sources can reduce muscle mass and block metabolism. A low protein intake also reduces the production of dopamine—a neurotransmitter that makes us feel satisfied, happy, and motivated.

Reducing carbohydrates too much can increase stress levels and reduce the production of serotonin—a neurotransmitter that makes us feel calm and relaxed. Restricting too much fat intake reduces the supply of the material with which the brain is built and destabilizes the transmission of nerve impulses.

Despite the confusion in the world of nutrition, the rules to follow are now apparent—eat a little less, abound with vegetables, choose whole grains only, take healthy proteins such as fish, eggs, lean meats, and legumes, use healthy fats such as extra virgin olive oil, avocados, nuts, and small amounts of butter, and try to use the one-course scheme proposed by Harvard University.

Fear of not coping when faced with a problem or challenge is something we all experience at some point in our lives. For some people, this becomes a limitation that prevents them from living to the fullest and hinders achieving their desired goals. No one likes to feel stuck, deprived by their inner limits of the freedom to act as best as possible and overcome the problems that come their way.

To prevent this from happening, we must have a strategic plan of action to take us out of the impasse. For many, it is helpful to have support and professional help to frame limits and resources and to create a path that leads to action and growth.

DECISION-MAKING FATIGUE

The more decisions we have to make, the more we experience decision-making fatigue, which almost always leads to us making bad choices.

Nowadays, even choosing which movie to watch can be complicated and exhausting. You spend a quarter of an hour scrolling through titles, maybe putting them on your favorites list, and then, feeling exhausted, decide to watch Friends for the umpteenth time.

The problem is not a lack of options but having too many. Every day, we are forced to make hundreds, if not thousands, of decisions. The white shirt or the blue shirt? Answer emails or work on the project? Make a casserole or an omelet?

Each of these decisions may seem irrelevant when made individually. But one after the other, they have a cumulative effect.

The more decisions we have to make, the more complicated it is to make them, and the more likely we will make the wrong ones. However, when you understand decision-making fatigue, you can structure your activities to avoid falling into it. The result will be a series of intelligent choices.

The ability to make good decisions is inversely proportional to the number of decisions we have to make.

To make a good decision, we need to weigh all the factors involved, decide what is most important, and then act on that analysis. But performing these calculations requires much mental energy.

One study showed the critical role that decision-making fatigue plays in making choices. Researchers looked at 1,112 probation judgments that took place over ten months. They wanted to determine what factors affected whether a judge would or would not grant probation to an offender. It turned out that the most discriminating factor was not the severity of the crime, nor the behavior in prison, but the time of day.

Judges were much more likely to grant probation early in the day and right after lunch. Why? At these two times, judges were, as they say, "fresher." They could easily weigh all the variables and make that decision. On the other hand, as the hours passed, fatigue set in, and they had difficulty evaluating the cases. Therefore, they leaned toward an automatic choice—no parole. Fewer choices mean fewer decisions. Can you, for example:

- Simplify your wardrobe, so you have fewer choices.
- Plan your meals at the beginning of the week.
- Create time blocks, so you know what tasks you'll be doing at any given time (e.g., 11 a.m. check mail).

The simpler your life becomes, the less you will struggle to make decisions.

Identify priorities

Knowing your priorities helps you to keep your focus on what matters most. It keeps you from having to decide what deserves your attention constantly. You can devote your energy to work rather than always deciding what to work on.

Make simple decisions in advance.

The more things you decide in advance, the less mental energy you need to spend at the moment. Try to make as many simple decisions in advance as you can by accumulating them. You can easily plan what to eat the next day (or the following week), what you'll wear, when you'll work out, etc.

Work on complex and important tasks first.

The more complex a task is, the more critical it is to work on it when fresh. As the hours of the day progress, your decision-making ability diminishes, and it will become increasingly difficult to have the motivation to tackle the challenging items on your list.

Fuel your body

This one should be obvious, but we often ignore it. Decision-making requires energy to function at maximum capacity, and you need to give your body the energy it needs. How? By eating at regular, healthy intervals and resting at night!

Eliminate distractions

As mentioned, distractions (especially digital ones) rob your attention and destroy your mental energy. Eliminating distractions is a great way to protect yourself from decision-making fatigue.

When managing decision-making fatigue, the goal is not to eliminate decisions. Instead, the goal is to have more energy available for the decisions that matter. Eliminate the unnecessary and dedicate yourself to the extraordinary.

REFRAIN FROM SUGARY FOOD OR JUNK

A diet too rich in processed, fatty, and sugary foods affects the function of the hippocampus—a part of the brain involved in memory and the modulation of appetite. It happens in mice and humans, as shown in a study published in the Royal Society Open Science. A group of healthy, normal-weight volunteers subjected to a week-long "Western diet" saturated with junk food reported difficulty remembering and exerting control over the hunger stimulus.

Previous research has established the ability of junk food to generate addiction, increase the desire for other unhealthy food, and interfere with hippocampus functions. But this is the first time both effects have been observed in humans and young, healthy individuals with no previous history of obesity.

When we see a bag of chips or a chocolate snack, the brain presents pleasant memories of the last time we ate this food. However, if we are complete, the hippocampus intervenes by suppressing these traces and momentarily dampening the desire for more food. This mechanism jams after a few days on a junk food diet.

For the study, researchers at Macquarie University and Griffith University in Australia recruited 110 slim, healthy volunteers in their 20s who were accustomed to a balanced, nutritious diet. Half of them switched menus for a week, gorging themselves on waffles, high-sugar cereals, and fast food lunches.

Before, during, and after this unpleasant dietary regimen, which made eight people give up the task early, they had to participate in memory assessment tests and questionnaires that explored their desire for junk food and appreciation for those obtained.

Those who had followed a diet rich in junk food showed reduced hippocampal function, visible in lower memory capacity and poorer self-control—these people craved junk food more than others. They remained hungry more often for the same number of calories consumed. Fortunately, the effect is reversible. The volunteers' memory and appetite returned to normal three weeks after returning to a regular diet. This is a sign that can counteract the negative influence of junk food on the hippocampus.

SPEND TIME JUST SITTING THERE

There is inevitably a time when our only desire is to put aside everything and be able to stop. But you don't have to wait for the much-dreamed-of vacations—every day, we can devote ourselves to what makes us feel good and help us recover the energy to keep going.

After a year of work, whether behind a desk or at home, of running here and there, of commitments, tasks, and concerns, we feel the vital need for a break from the usual hellish rhythms. To finally be able to stop on the shore of a sunny beach or the top of a mountain does not matter, the important thing is to get a break.

But do we have to wait for the moment of the longed-for vacation to put aside our hectic lives and enjoy a few moments of rest and well-being?

The fundamental problem is that life doesn't stop. If we need to rest, there are still things we must do: we must continue to work, produce, and meet commitments and deadlines, even though we have little strength. But if life doesn't stop, can we stop? While waiting for the vacation, is it possible to carve out moments of relaxation from everyday life? Can we find spaces and moments of rest to immerse ourselves in recharging, just enough to restore and take a breath?

Perhaps it is. It is possible to take time for ourselves and find the energy that can sustain us when we feel we no longer have the strength. But what can we do concretely to recharge ourselves?

We have things we like (and theoretically make us feel good) and things we don't like but unfortunately have to do. The situation becomes much heavier to bear if, beyond fatigue and lack of energy, our lives are unbalanced mainly towards the things that must be done, with little or no room for activities that can produce beneficial effects on us.

Since we are all different, it is impossible to list all the activities that make us feel good. Each of us knows what we like and don't like, what makes us feel alive or productive, and what restores our energy or, more significantly, serenity.

So, the first step is pretty simple… take a pen and paper and write down at least five activities that are a source of pleasure and joy for you, or restore a sense of effectiveness and productivity. It is better if these activities embody both characteristics, but finding such "complete" ones is difficult. If you're having trouble finding them, below are some ideas that I hope will be helpful to you.

Often, these activities allow us to immerse ourselves at that moment, putting aside fatigue, thoughts, and tasks. They are easy to find if we look for them among our interests, the things we enjoy. For example:

- Reading a book
- Taking a walk in nature
- Taking a trip out of town

- Writing a poem, letter, or story
- Eating an ice cream
- Playing with your children (or with a four-legged friend)

We can also sit, enjoying our presence, and listening to our breathing. Whether the vacations are near or far away, impossible or already over, we can find ways to temporarily unplug and recharge our batteries simply by devoting time to ourselves and what we enjoy most.

First, we need to identify at least five activities that suit us (more, if we feel like it), then we need to decide when, where, and possibly with who to do them. This, perhaps, is the most challenging part—finding the time to devote to ourselves when we think there is no time.

In reality, this is a real investment. Even a few minutes to devote to what makes us feel good can give us more energy, an improved mood, and better relationships. Therefore, it is not a question of the quantity of time "lost" but the quality of time "gained."

STAY FOCUSED ON YOUR ONE THING UNTIL YOU ARE FINISHED.

In the age of fast communication, multi-tasking, and on-demand entertainment, the ability to concentrate is increasingly rare. We are so accustomed to constant interruptions in our work that we can only focus for long periods if distracted.

Unlike concentration, multitasking is not a superpower. Dividing one's mental energy into many activities does not allow us to go deep into them. To concentrate on one activity means to devote all our attention to it without allowing other thoughts or needs to divert it from our goal.

First, it is necessary to identify our general objective. For some, it may be to study for an exam and write a thesis for others to develop a work project. We need to tell our brain what its focus will be. We can have more than one goal; we can have many. But every moment, we must focus on just one of them without getting lost in thinking about others.

Once we have established our general objective, we need to go into more detail and focus on the mini-objectives, those bricks that make up the general objective. We must dedicate ourselves to each session of deep work for each of these mini-goals, giving all of ourselves to achieve it. We concentrate only when the activity absorbs our mental energy. Completing one of these small goals motivates us to attack the second, the third, and so on, creating a virtuous circle of motivation and concentration.

Deep and dedicated work allows us to do our best by focusing on a single goal without distractions. If we continuously train ourselves for more extended periods, success will be short in coming, whatever our goal.

But deciding to focus is not enough… we must take action. To do this, we must plan our work sessions and protect them from distractions. Concentration will allow us to get high marks in our exams by studying quickly, learning foreign languages, playing the guitar, and doing any other activity with profit. Concentration is the way of life of people who appear good at everything.

Thanks to the productive efficiency that concentration allows us to achieve, we have much free time to devote to leisure activities, social life, and pure relaxation.

"Keep moving ahead because action creates momentum, which in turn creates unanticipated opportunities."

—Nick Vujicic

4

HOW TO BUILD MASSIVE MOMENTUM

Have you ever been completely and fully dedicated to a goal? Have you ever gotten so lost in your work that you lost track of time? Unaware of the outside world, focused only on your progress and what's happening here and now? Think about it... it probably happened to you while you were doing something you're passionate about.

If you answered "yes" to any of these questions, chances are you've experienced momentum. This state is one of the keys to happiness at work and in your personal life, and one of its side benefits is that it not only reduces stress but increases productivity by leaps and bounds. It's a state of mind that roots us entirely in the present moment and helps us be more creative, productive, and happy.

In this chapter, we'll explain in detail how to develop momentum, why it's essential, and how to achieve it to increase productivity and happiness toward your goals. Building momentum in your life is about improving the things that drive you forward and decreasing the things that hold you back. It sounds like a no-brainer, but I know, just like you, that living the life we desire isn't always easy. We have habits and repeated cycles to overcome. But by building momentum, we can break through them and move into the life we want.

Momentum, by its nature, takes an initial push to get the ball rolling. Here are 12 tips to jumpstart the speed in your life:

DO ONE SMALL TASK EVERYDAY

We gain a fundamental psychological advantage when we create and establish small steps to take every day. First, we set a goal that is not scary but achievable in an "easy" way. This keeps us calm instead of raising negative thoughts and risking blocking everything. Imagine an "untrained" person who decides to run a marathon. As soon as he thinks about this goal, he becomes paralyzed and thinks, "I have to run 42.195 km, not even for all the gold in the world!"

But if instead, our goal was divided into incremental steps and intermediate tests, the same would be feasible and, therefore, would not trigger any alarm. Breaking tasks into small, repetitive actions is the secret to achieving ambitious goals.

TAKE ON A MONTHLY CHALLENGE

The 30-day challenges are among my favorite methods of personal development and improvement. They are based on a straightforward concept—it takes 21 days for an activity to become a habit. Do the challenges work? It sometimes depends on permanently instilling a habit, especially if it is distant from our current conception; it takes longer. Still, despite this, a 30-day challenge can be beneficial to:

- Open your mind
- Try new activities
- Overcome your limits (and understand how far you can go)
- Know yourself better

- Train self-discipline
- Prove to yourself that you can be consistent
- Get out of your comfort zone

The first time I approached 30-day challenges was with fitness goals. We're all familiar with squat challenges, running challenges, ab challenges, and so on. It wasn't until later that I discovered that the model could easily be applied to many other areas, and the world opened up to me. I usually track the progress of challenges in my bullet journal, which helps keep motivation high and reinforces consistency.

If your goal is to establish a new habit rather than to test yourself in a shorter time frame, I recommend five-day challenges. A shorter period will allow us to measure ourselves nimbly and in smaller tasks without prolonging them for a month.

TAKE ACTION IN THE FACE OF FEAR

Many people ask me, "I'm stuck in fear; how can I overcome this? I'm afraid I'll never find the perfect partner or reach my dream goal." The first thing to remember is that we all have fears.

What differentiates people who always seem to be able to overcome fears from those who are paralyzed by fear is not how afraid we are but how much we know about that fear and how we choose to respond to it. You see, most of our concerns stem from a protective mechanism triggered when we are challenged to reduce any possible risk of "failing" or "falling".

Fear tries to keep you safe, but it does so by shifting your focus to the negative aspects of change and urging you to avoid taking risks. Of course, there are certain risks that we should avoid.

But when this protective mechanism prevents you from taking the actions necessary to live the life you want and realize your plans, it's time to learn how to overcome fear, or rather, how to act despite fear. This is the only way to get closer to your dreams, and there are no shortcuts.

In all likelihood, that unattainable goal you set will be less terrible than you thought. Suppose you believe fear is one of your giant demons. In that case, I suggest you check out my book, *Nothing Scares Me: Charge Forward with Confidence, Conquer Resistance, and Break Through Your Limitations* to go deeper into the subject and defeat fear forever.

ADDRESS ISSUES AROUND PROCRASTINATION

One of the leading causes of procrastination is the lack of the right incentive to begin a particular task. Newton's first principle of dynamics is as follows, "Everybody perseveres in its state of stillness or uniform rectilinear motion unless it is forced to change that state by forces applied to it."

If you tend to procrastinate, you are like an object in its state of stillness. When you start working on a project, you become a moving object, even if it's just getting started. As we said earlier, to stop procrastinating, all you need to do is start. The impetus that leads you to start is like the force that guides the object in a state of stillness to change its shape.

A great way to put this principle into practice is to start with a small part of the task you need to tackle. This momentum will give you the impetus to keep working on your project. If you have to do a task that you tend to put off often and for a long time, put it as your first task the next day. Starting without distractions and the usual routine will allow you to stop overthinking and take action. Getting started will gratify you enough to keep going.

CONTROL YOUR DISTRACTIONS

How many times did you check your phone today? How many emails did you answer during a business meeting? Digital distraction is one of the greatest enemies of productivity because it interferes with concentration and continuity at work. Entrepreneurs, professionals, and managers all suffer from a distraction syndrome that leads to not being focused on the required task.

The distraction involves a significant expenditure of energy in resuming what you do after each interruption. Productivity suffers, and you feel like you haven't accomplished anything despite being exhausted at the end of the workday. Distractions are challenging to overcome but not impossible. After you become aware of the habit, some changes in behavior will help detox, with great benefit to your productivity.

COMMIT TO A 30-MINUTE MORNING ROUTINE

Creating an effective 30-minute morning routine can help you develop a great frame of mind to start your day.

You can do many things in the morning to improve mental flexibility and alertness. If you're not a morning person or like to keep hitting the "snooze" button on your alarm clock, we have just the thing for you. I am increasingly convinced that how we spend the early morning hours can influence the rest of our day, especially when developing a morning routine. During this time of day, our minds are fresh and clear of the challenges that life has in store for us and, therefore, open and able to improve our entire day dramatically.

We can use this time to work on a project that has been in the drawer for a long time, spend time with family, learn to focus through mindfulness, or learn to enjoy a good cup of coffee!

People who get up early tend to anticipate problems and do their best to minimize them, which helps them get more done in their studies and business opportunities. In fact, by getting up early, you can get ready for the day rather than chasing all the tasks right away.

BLOCK IN YOUR ACTION TASK

Do you ever get to the end of the day dead tired but feeling like you didn't get the day organized? It sounds crazy, I know. Yet that's what happens when you waste precious energy because of disorganization, mainly due to poor time management.

Until recently, this happened to me a lot. I couldn't focus on one thing; I filled my schedule with tasks I struggled to accomplish. Each job took me longer than it should have, and I constantly felt I needed to catch up on everything. This is a steady building of frustration, nervousness, and dissatisfaction in all aspects of my life.

At some point, I realized I couldn't keep this up, and I had to find a way to organize my day better if I wanted to get results. One strategy that has helped me manage my day is setting times to work without interruptions. Blocks can be 15, 30, 45, or 90 minutes long—you decide based on your pace and needs.

No distractions of any kind are allowed during these sessions. The reason is straightforward… if you keep interrupting what you're doing, you'll get nowhere (and feel exhausted anyway). Don't let others dictate your time; you decide how to use it.

FOCUS: ONLY ONE PRIORITY TASK PER DAY

Although not of the utmost importance, we all have several things to manage that still need to be completed. And I'm not just talking about work stuff, but also activities that involve our free time. A key aspect of being more productive is focusing on a specific task.

Plan the tasks according to the closest deadline or delivery date and consider the most important ones to complete. For example, if you have a project due in a short period, this will probably be your highest priority task for the next few days. Similarly, studying a subject will likely be at the top of your to-do list if you have a university exam in a week or two.

Multitasking is best left to computers, whereas humans are most efficient when focusing on one thing at a time. If you think about it, the meaning of planning your work by dedicating a certain amount of time to each thing is to put in sequence the things you have to do to tackle them one at a time!

REVIEW YOUR GOALS TWICE A DAY

The world is divided into two categories—people who dream and think about their future but struggle to get there and create it, and those who instead have a concrete idea of where they want to go. Step by step, manage your tasks in a way that will allow you to achieve your goals. With that in mind, I want to share a technique that has helped me tremendously.

The technique involves imagining yourself feeling the emotions you expect to feel once you reach your goal, experiencing them with intensity at least twice a day; I suggest morning and evening.

You can do this technique by associating it to the same criteria with which you practice meditation (so a quiet place, with eyes closed, relaxed, and start to evoke those images of you once the goal is reached, at least twice a day). This is an exercise of training the brain, and our emotional capacity will become more and more effective at producing that high-definition film.

One day, it will be that very film that gives you the driving energy because you say, *"Damn, it's there, I feel it, I live that situation, I feel it inside me, and as I can reproduce it inside me, I will be able to create it in reality."*

GET ONE SMALL WIN PER DAY

Two main factors motivate human beings—decreased pain and increased pain. The more something gives you joy, the more your brain will want it. The more a thing causes you pain, the less you will be inclined to do it. Would you prefer to do something you enjoy or something you don't want? The answer seems obvious. However, how can you do the things that, at first glance, you don't like? Simple: by making them enjoyable!

At the beginning of each week, define a prize, which you can collect only once you have completed all your tasks for that day. This can be an activity you'd like to do that you no longer allow yourself to do or something you've always wanted to do but didn't feel you deserved.

Did you accomplish all the tasks you defined for today? Great. Treat yourself to your reward. Isn't it nice to be able to enjoy life a little? This will keep you motivated to accomplish more in the weeks to come!

GO THE EXTRA MILE

There are times when moving forward seems impossible when we're confident we've scraped the bottom of our reserves, but it's precisely in these moments that we should remember the 40% rule. This is a straightforward tool, but I hope to help you rethink your limitations.

Newt Gingrich, an American politician, said, "Perseverance is the hard work you do after all the hard work you've already done." It's a phrase that captures the true essence of perseverance and determination. The 40% rule is applied by the famous Navy Seals (U.S. Navy Special Forces), known for the rather demanding physical training that takes them to the limits of their capabilities.

According to these soldiers, we can endure much more than we think and go beyond what we set out to do. According to them, when our mind says, "Enough," we have only reached 40% of our potential. Therefore, when we are about to throw in the towel, we can continue and strive 60% harder.

The 40% rule is a straightforward tool that helps us re-evaluate our limits and allows us to change our perspective. It teaches us that if we want to push our boundaries, we need to take a step further and show our brain that this barrier is just a figment of our imagination.

Over the next few days, you'll feel like giving up and trading your goals for some cheap distraction on at least one occasion. However, when one of those occasions arises, I'd like you to remember the 40% rule. But most of all, I'd like you to peek beyond what you think your limits are today instead of giving up on the first few difficulties. Just a peek. A small step over the fence. Nothing more.

TAKE MASSIVE ACTION ONE DAY A WEEK

The search for one's vocation is a process that is sometimes long and full of contingencies; goals, on the other hand, are different. If work is a drive of the soul, you choose plans that may be short-term. You may dream of traveling the world, you feel it's your calling, but you might still want to learn how to surf.

So, in a year, you might achieve several goals but choose not to pursue them in the following year. It's part of life experience. Also, completing a plan is such a rewarding thing to do that it boosts your self-esteem.

Once you've defined your goals, you must figure out how to devote daily time to achieve them. Whether you're the president of NATO or an ordinary citizen, you get the same number of hours in a day. To make the most of them, you must live every moment to the fullest. You must rest well and deeply, eat food that gives you energy and not take it away. You must eliminate all bad habits and replace them with good ones.

Dedicate one day of the week to concentrate on reaching your goal. Not only will it allow you to accomplish necessary tasks, but it will also give you a boost of self-esteem to perform your everyday work on the following days.

If you need more time to stay focused, try starting with 10 minutes, then take a break and resume for another 10 minutes. The time is right; without realizing it, you will have worked for two hours on your project. Remember, action is the essential key to seeing our dreams come true. You can spend your whole life properly planning your ambitious goal, but it will only happen once you start taking action.

5
TAKE MASSIVE ACTION ON YOUR GOALS

Any personal growth book you read emphasizes the importance of planning your life in detail, setting your goals, and drafting an action plan to achieve them. I've been discovering the world of personal growth for several years, and I should have written my goals immediately.

So, don't make the same mistake! Instead, do all the exercises I recommend in this chapter. Living without having clear goals is like driving in thick fog. No matter how fast your car is or how perfect the road you're on is, you're forced to move slowly and make very little progress toward your destination.

Before we get into the chapter, I want to bring you back to a fascinating study to understand the importance of having goals. In 1979, researchers asked a class of Harvard undergraduates if they had written down clear goals for the future and made plans to achieve them.

Only 3% of the students had written goals and planned to achieve them, and 13% had dreams, but the best results always emerged from putting goals down on paper. Instead, the remaining 84% had no plans other than finishing school and enjoying their summer vacation.

Ten years later, in 1989, the researchers surveyed members of the same class again. The 13% of students had goals but had yet to put them in writing and earned twice as much as the

84% of students with no purpose whatsoever. However, the most surprising finding was that the 3% of students who had dreams and plans to achieve them and had put them in writing earned, on average, ten times as much as the remaining 97%. That's a staggering statistic.

THE IMPORTANCE OF SETTING GOALS

It is crucial to have goals because "happiness is the progressive realization of a goal or noble ideal." This is one of the best definitions of happiness. I experience it every single day in my life. When I work on myself, trying to impersonate my ideals, I am satisfied and feel a great sense of self-worth.

Instead, when I make the easy choice of not sacrificing myself in the present to create a better future, I feel sad and don't esteem myself. Remember, the greatest need of every human being is to have a future goal to look forward to, to give meaning and purpose to their life, and to provide strength to face the difficulties of the present.

We are happy when our actions are congruent with our values. Therefore, your values must be in accord with your goals, and your goals must agree with your values. The more your behavior in the present is consistent with the behavior you deem ideal, the more respect and esteem you have for yourself. Living your life in disagreement with your values is an effective strategy for experiencing stress, negativity, unhappiness, and frustration. As Abram Maslow argues, "A man must become all that he can be."

To find out your values, ask yourself what makes you feel necessary. What actions boost your self-esteem? What accomplishments have you achieved in the past that made you proud of yourself? How would you like to be remembered when you are gone? In my case, knowledge, wisdom, discovery, and creativity are values I can't live without.

SHORT-TERM VS. LONG-TERM

Once you've clarified your values, you need to write a detailed vision of your long-term future to ensure you make the right choices in the present. What do you want your ideal life to look like 10, 20, 30, or 40 years from now? When answering this question, please don't limit yourself; answer it by describing what you want in the various areas of your life in a particular way.

What work would you like to do? How much money would you like to earn? How would you like to spend your free time? What will your family be like? What friendships will you have? What is your ideal level of physical and mental health? You must not exclude any aspect that constitutes a balanced life because, if you do, just like a wheel out of proportion, your life will not flow properly.

Once you have imagined and written down your ideal life in detail, bring your attention back to the present and start planning, day by day, the actions that will be necessary for you to materialize it. However, please take your time to achieve your goal. Thinking that you can earn a million in a year is unrealistic if you don't have a penny in your pocket. When you find out that you won't reach your goal, you will feel unmotivated, and you will be more inclined to abandon your plans for the future altogether.

Therefore, it is essential to divide your goals into smaller ones within your reach, bringing you closer and closer to your main objective in the long run. Most people overestimate what they can do in one year and underestimate what they can do in five years, ten years, or 20 years.

The Goal Is the King; The Motivation Is the Queen

Many of you have probably set goals in the past, perhaps the so-called "New Year's resolutions" that you have not achieved. Year after year, the same pattern repeats itself... you start down a particular path to reach your goals, but then, along the way, you lose motivation, and it all comes to nothing.

Have you ever wondered what this constant lack of success in achieving your annual resolutions is? One possible answer is that you are not motivated to work toward them. Let me give you an example. Let's say your goal is to lose weight because you want to go to the beach in the summer to show off an excellent, lean physique. You could go on a diet for a few days or weeks.

Then you start to eat out... first one day, then another, until you go back to eating the way you did before you went on a diet. You remain at the same weight or maybe even gain weight because of the psycho-physiological compensation due to the caloric deficit previously maintained for a few weeks (it is not uncommon for those who diet for a certain period to regain the pounds lost with interest). Such situations occur every day.

Let me give you another example. Let's say that the life of someone you love (for example, your mother or father, your wife or husband, etc.) depends solely on your dieting and exercising every day until you achieve a lean and fit physique. What would you do? I'll tell you... you would diet and exercise without even thinking about it, and most importantly, you would achieve your goal with a 100% chance of success.

Can you see the different approach? So, what is stopping you from achieving your goals? The fact that you need more motivation or that you need more reasons!

HOW TO DEFINE YOUR GOALS WITH THE "HANDS TECHNIQUE"

Now that you know how your mind behaves regarding goals, you have a valuable strategy in your hands.

You are no longer unprepared but can define and achieve your goals by being aware of these mental dynamics. Let's get practical!

In this article, we will focus on defining the goals that are important to you. Specifically, we will use the hand technique. Each finger represents a dream with particular importance in the hand's approach, and the finger's length gives the significance of each plan.

If you think about it, it is a perfect system. With the hand technique, we will have to define two critical goals for us—four medium-important goals and four relatively unimportant goals. Ultimately, we will have ten objectives—10 is the perfect number for defining essential goals. There are not too many or too few, and they allow you to plan appropriately and do well-distributed work.

Remember that as far as the two high-priority goals are concerned, these are the things that are important to you. In your notebook or on a piece of paper, write the title "Long-Term Goals." In this step, you need to answer the following question, "What do I want to accomplish in my life in X years?"

Since these are long-term goals, you need to consider them as goals that you want to accomplish within a specific time frame, which can be one to 10 years or even longer (depending on the magnitude of your plan). Remember one key thing: be detailed! It would help if you clearly described what you want to achieve.

For example, if you want a specific job, describe the type of work, the tasks you would like to do, the salary you would like to receive, the responsibilities, how many employees you would like to manage, and so on. The goal is to understand precisely what you want.

Once you have completed this step, you need to move on to the next one—motivation.

Why do you want to achieve that particular goal? This step is crucial because, by analyzing your desire for achievement, you may find that it is not that important for you to accomplish that specific goal.

This would then prompt you to revisit the goal, find a new one, or create a new plan. On the contrary, your reasons for achieving that goal are vitally important. The bottom line is that if you have valid reasons for achieving your plan, you will have a better chance of achieving it. Conversely, frivolous motives may cause you to fail. Remember that the more critical and significant the goal, the more you must have valid and vital reasons for achieving it.

12 STEPS TO DEFINING YOUR GOALS

One of the best ways to increase my productivity is to write my main goal of the day at the top of my planner page as soon as I wake up. Once I've done that, I list in order of importance the actions I need to take that particular day to get closer to my main goal at that specific stage of my life.

By doing so, my daily actions are always congruent with my future goal. This simple exercise is invaluable; I recommend applying it as early as tomorrow. Here's a 12-step process for defining your goals:

1. The first step is to have a desire that makes you excited just thinking about it. To achieve what you want, you must have a deep passion; otherwise, you will need more motivation to tackle the difficulties you encounter.

2. The second step is to believe that you can achieve your goal because if you don't think you can, you won't make any effort to change your situation. The belief in yourself will improve with every action you take; the closer you get to what you want, the more you will believe your goal is within your reach.
3. The third step is to put your goal in writing. A plan not set in writing is not a goal but a simple preference. If you want to achieve big goals, you need to start writing them down.
4. The fourth step is to determine your starting point to set goals within reach and avoid making the mistake of aiming too high right out of the gate.
5. The fifth step is to determine why you want to achieve your goal and write it down. What benefits will you have? What benefits will your loved ones have? Don't just write down one or two reasons; try to write down as many as possible. If you have 30 or 40 reasons why you want to achieve a specific goal, you will be less inclined to throw in the towel at times of difficulty because you will know exactly why you started your journey in the first place.
6. The sixth step is to identify a date in the future when you set out again to achieve what you want. However, you should only demoralize yourself if you meet the time limit, and in that case, you'll need to pick a more suitable date and refocus.
7. The seventh step is to identify the obstacles separating you from your goal, what habits you will need to change, and why you still need to accomplish your desire.
8. The eighth step is to determine the skills and information you will need to learn; for example, if you want to become

an actor, it would be a good idea to enroll in an acting class or improve your diction. A good question to ask yourself is, "What new skills can I learn to help me achieve my goal?"
9. The ninth step is to determine what people you will need around you. You will need to learn to collaborate with others to achieve anything significant.
10. The 10th step is to draw up an action plan; a plan is a list of actions you'll need to complete to get from where you are to where you want to be. You should combine all the previous steps and determine what actions you will need to take.
11. The 11th step is to visualize your goal often as if you have already achieved it; this will help you overcome any limiting beliefs you may have.
12. The 12th step is not to give up! If your goal is fundamental before you start working on it, you must promise yourself that no matter your problems or difficulties, you will persevere until you achieve it.

At this point, you have clarified your goals and motivations. Now you need to create an action plan. In this plan, you will write down the steps necessary to achieve your goals. Please write them down according to a clear priority (most important things to do first) and sequence. Each point in your action plan represents a step forward in achieving your goal.

This is a crucial step—creating the strategy to guide you toward achieving your goal. Take your time, revise it, correct it, update it, and above all, follow it. Day after day, month after month, complete each item on the list, from the first to the last. Only in this way will you achieve your goal.

"While a good leader sustains momentum, a great leader increases it."

—John C. Maxwell

6

SETTING THE STAGE FOR MASSIVE ACTION

I often see people trying to achieve a goal but needing help knowing how to do it. Sometimes, they put in counterproductive place behaviors, leaving them frustrated and failing. In many cases, although there is a genuine desire to change certain aspects of their lives, what is missing is the will, motivation, and ability to channel these efforts in the right way.

Do you want to know the secrets successful people use that you can use immediately? Want to learn how to transform your life and make it better? This chapter will teach you the five elements of taking action and pushing forward. It starts with having a specific plan, showing up to work on your project, and committing to a consistent stream of progress for the long term.

PLANNING

First, identify your why. This is your compelling reason for taking on any challenge. Without a purpose guiding you like a compass, your action plans will fail to fulfill you, and you may struggle to maintain motivation. What is the why behind your goal? What changes will take place in your life when you reach this goal?

The why is a reason aligned with you and the person you want to become—it's never a matter of lack of will or time.

Think back to when you got something you wanted… the time, energy, and dedication were there, and nothing could stop you.

"You shouldn't get to the top of the ladder only to find that it was leaning against the wrong wall."

Those who pursue goals that align with their values feel more satisfied and fulfilled. When we achieve a goal following our values, i.e., what we believe in and think is truly important to us, we experience a burst of energy and feel mentally and emotionally fulfilled. Only with this awareness can you move on to define your professional and personal goals systematically and methodically.

Mistakes are often made at this stage because many must set goals and plan them effectively. Let's look at some pointers so that you can immediately put them into practice and start deciding what you want in your professional and personal life.

"Successful people are ordinary people with successful habits."
—Bryan Tracy.

Bryan Tracy is a respected expert in personal and professional development, efficiency, and coaching. He has written numerous best-selling books and is among the hottest trainers/consultants in professional growth. Bryan Tracy analyzed what enabled people to achieve their goals and identified crucial habits, behaviors, and attitudes. One of the habits every day in these people was the ability to plan effectively for what they wanted to achieve. First, it is best to distinguish between these two types of goals:

RESULT GOALS

A result goal is to achieve a particular result (for example, acquiring 20 new customers or losing 5kg of weight). These goals can motivate and focus our attention positively on what we will achieve.

PROCESS GOALS

A process goal (e.g., make three business visits a day or exercise every day for 20 minutes) focuses on the present and not on the future, learning and acquiring a method, i.e., a habit! The advantage of these goals is that we focus on the small steps that need to be done daily. You can start slow and acquire healthy, functional habits.

Is it easier to think about 20 minutes a day of physical activity or lose 10 pounds? The power of process goals is acquiring a habit and taking action immediately! Which can be challenging! It helps you get organized and set aside time every day for yourself and the commitment you've made to yourself. Here are the six steps to planning your goals:

Step 1: Decide clearly what you want, and be as specific as possible: "I would like to increase my business and gain 20 new clients within a year." This is specific, and it already indicates the strategy and next steps.

Step 2: Write your goals down: It is part of the planning process. According to Bryan Tracy, writing down and re-reading our goals can sometimes make a difference. I have for years had my study filled with mind maps and strategic goals I want to achieve so that I can monitor them periodically.

Step 3: Make them measurable: Use numbers to make your goals measurable. Within your goal setting, verify that there is a number, a figure, and ask yourself, "What is the number that will tell me I have achieved this goal?" It will be much easier to stay focused.

Step 4: Set a deadline, and define intermediate deadlines if necessary: When do you want to achieve that goal? What is the first step? When will you take action?

Step 5: Make a list of all the things you need to do:

- Problems and obstacles between you and your goals
- Knowledge and skills you will need
- People whose cooperation you will need
- Turn the list into a plan
- Priorities? What are the steps and the most critical actions?
- Sequence? In what order should they be done?

Step 6: Act immediately; start right away with the first step. This is the power of immediate action that triggers the process of accomplishing your goals. Whenever you decide on a plan, make a decision, and take a small step toward those goals immediately. It's the way to convince our minds that we mean business.

TESTING

At this point, it is helpful to consider the issue of "getting involved." It is a concept that, at first glance, is very psychological, involving aspects such as courage, will, determination to pursue a goal, and commitment to achieve it.

Upon careful analysis, we realize there is a much broader parallelism in this regard. It is not limited to including the human being as an entity but ranges from nature itself to the dimension of life. Getting involved can be an objective synonym for evolution, movement, and renunciation of stagnation.

Many times, in choosing to undertake a path or an activity, even a simple one, we are blocked at an unconscious level by beliefs rooted in our mind or limiting fears, which push us to stay in our comfort zone and, consequently, backtrack in progress made.

In this sense, giving up growth to keep us in a safe zone makes us lose familiarity with the ability to try, making us more vulnerable to failure and increasing pre-existing fears, which are magnified precisely because they are never disconfirmed. It is only possible to expect that, once a result is obtained, it will remain stable over time with regular maintenance. This can be seen in the body's structure and physical training, but in any manual practice that has not been done for a long time. In essence, those who do not stay active lose responsiveness and efficiency.

Accepting change and life's challenges as necessary can be the key to learning to take advantage of all the opportunities for evolution we encounter while giving up fear.

In short, it's never too late to start something—no external judgment should influence what is most suitable for us.

In addition, a suitable challenge encourages us to try again in case of failure because we have the awareness that it is within our reach, and we will, therefore, be driven to growth by the mere fact of trying to correct our mistakes.

The mistake often made in the process of evolution is to move too suddenly from a zone of comfort to an area of panic, where we tend to encounter difficulties. Starting from zero and trying to conquer the world from one day to the next often generates a recession because we need the right tools to handle the unexpected and be sufficiently trained to withstand the inevitable setbacks.

FAILING

Want to create a million-dollar company? Fine, but it's essential to understand that it may not work out for a long time.

Want to become a singer acclaimed by thousands? Great, then know that between you and the day thousands of people come to hear you, there will be a concert with very few people, including your parents, your brothers/sisters, and that aunt you haven't seen in years.

Want to write a bestseller? Great, but know that there will probably be 20 books that won't sell between book one and your first bestseller.

You will have to encounter setbacks and difficulties to achieve any goal. It doesn't have to be that way, but you should consider the possibility. There is no successful person who has not had to overcome challenges.

The idea of success that society gives us is false. We are taught that success is the opposite of failure, but if you want to succeed in something, you must learn to see every problem as an opportunity to grow. You have to learn to see defeat as a teacher. There is no such thing as overnight success. What the media does is sell the idea of easy success. Want sculpted abs? Here's the super-powerful pill that shapes your abdomen in five days. Society convinces us that we can have it all right away, but we can't. You can achieve your dreams and goals, but you must learn to keep your enthusiasm high despite the various defeats you will face.

When we encounter difficulties in life, we are given a chance to reach a higher level. We are allowed to improve. True success has nothing to do with overnight success but much with daily improvement.

Here is an example of a successful person: He ran for office in 1840, 1843, 1848, 1849, 1854, 1856 (where he took very few votes), and 1858. And after this list of defeats at all levels (local elections, party primaries, regional elections), he finally won in 1860... as President of the USA! I'm talking about Abraham Lincoln. Imagine if he hadn't tried again. Imagine if, after the first attempt, he had given up.

Here's another example: Soichiro Honda worked in his home garage to create snap rings to sell to Toyota. Initially, Toyota rejected his designs, but later, when they accepted, his factory was almost totally razed due to wartime bombing.

By the war's end, Honda was so poor that he could not even buy fuel to drive the car. However, he asked himself a compelling question, "How can I use the things I already have to get to where I want to go?" So, he noticed a small motor and got the idea to mount it on his bicycle. That's when he created the first motorized bicycle, which he called the Honda Dream Type A. Two years later, in 1948, the Honda Motor Company was born.

If you study and analyze the lives of successful people, you will realize how many challenges they had to overcome before they reached their goals. An important concept you need to remember is that by working on yourself, every day, you will bridge a little gap between the person you are and the person you want to become. You can achieve your dreams, but you must believe in them.

You have to take responsibility for making it happen without pointing fingers at anyone and making excuses. You will encounter setbacks that will only become permanent if you see them as such. Give yourself other opportunities—do more auditions, keep looking for a publishing house that believes in you, and create another company. Learn from every "failure." After every mistake, stop and understand what you need to do better and where to improve.

Change the strategy but not the goal. People don't achieve their goals mainly because they give up as soon as the first hurdles come. True emotional, financial, spiritual, and physical growth happens by overcoming what we used to consider our limitations. The only people who don't have problems are the ones in the cemetery.

Whatever your goal is, it is likely that you will face challenges and setbacks on your way to achieving it. So, learn from every single event in your life. What if you develop that mindset that brings confidence even when no one believes in you? When your goal seems unattainable because of so many consecutive failures, you keep telling yourself, "I will find a way to make my dream come true."

Successful people often fail, and losers fail often. So, what's the difference?

Successful people continue until they reach their goals. Others, after the first few attempts, give up. They are not willing to be told "no," to look for new and better strategies, they can't handle the frustration, so they quit, not knowing that with a little more effort, they could probably succeed. You don't give up; keep the focus and fight to achieve a goal that is important to you.

TRYING BEFORE READY

Successful people act before they feel ready and learn by doing. Most people, on the other hand, do just the opposite.

When you have an idea, take action. What you need, you will learn as you go. Prepare as best as possible in a short period, and then act. Only action can turn an idea into something tangible. The new mantra might be "ready, fire, aim."

When you start something new, it's normal not to know everything about it, but you don't need to. The helpful thing is understanding the bare minimum, so you can take action and figure out where you're going wrong. Everything you'll need, you'll figure out as you go along. Remember that you learn by making mistakes.

There is no time when you will feel ready for the essential things, but you will have to act anyway. Jim Rohn beautifully expressed this concept in a beautiful phrase: "You don't have to be great to start. But you do have to start to become great."

It is so important to step out of your comfort zone. For example, if you are used to speaking to 300 people but are asked to talk to an audience of 9,000, you will not feel up to it. But if you decide to talk to them anyway, you will begin to realize that you can do it and increase the area in which you feel comfortable.

Despite your mind finding a thousand excuses not to, this ability to take action is a skill you need to develop. What action can you take today that you have been putting off for so long? What do you know you should do but are putting off because of fear? Start to get into the healthy habit of doing the things that scare you and start taking action even when you don't feel ready.

COMMITTING TO THE LONG-TERM PATH

Most of our imagery of success is superficial, linked to many stereotypes that only exalt the concept of victory rather than building a victory; how a person can achieve success coincides with achieving a goal. Another great obsession is that of wanting to be considered "winners."

How many achievements make us winners? Success is, first and foremost, a mental attitude that influences our behaviors in every area of our lives. Coaching, flexibility, and the ability to adapt oneself to control the context are the foundations of any winning approach.

Emotions influence our behaviors and have a decisive impact on our performance. You don't need to be a business expert to understand that those who are moved by a deep love for their activity and live their profession with joy and fun can infect their colleagues, collaborators, and clients with positive energy. Emotional competencies are essential to nurturing this "operational happiness" and performance.

Often, the losers are those who give up when faced with difficulties and obstacles because they are unprepared to deal with them. On the other hand, the losers often did not have the emotional tools to read the implicit signals of the context and were faced with unexpected suffering.

Coaching excellent behaviors means helping people direct their energies to consistent goals.

It means questioning and interrogating one's expectations to always align with us and the relationship with the client. Once excellent behavior has been established, you must repeat the behavior with perseverance; we must nurture our professionalism with consistency. Relationships must also be encouraged—you cannot give up on your first or second attempt at contact. We cannot be defeated by a superficial attitude toward the people we relate to.

Building an opportunity means investing your skills to the highest potential. I believe the most significant thing is to make your dreams come true. Cultivating them is an activity we always do with joy and total involvement. Often, once our dreams are realized, we are nostalgic for the path we took to achieve them.

Realizing your big goals means abandoning the myopic vision and dedicating yourself (for the long term) to transform all your dreams into lifelong memories.

> *"The most important thing you can do to achieve your goals is to make sure that as soon as you set them you immediately begin to create momentum."*

—Tony Robbins

7

DEVELOPING THE ACTION MINDSET

What would you say if we asked what a person's success depends on? You might say it's a matter of talent, intelligence, or education. For some, the best place to start is by counting on good opportunities. Beyond everything, having the right mindset is the key to everything. It seems naive to think that "want is power," but I'm pretty clear about that. There's much uncertainty behind this topic, so we'll study the five critical elements of developing a mindset devoted to action in this chapter. Let's first look at what the word philosophy means.

Our mentality or mindset is our beliefs about how the world and ourselves work. Based on this, we regulate our behavior. Therefore, what we take for granted leads us to act in one way or another, ultimately determining our outcomes.

I came to this conclusion after observing a group of four-year-olds faced with the following dilemma—solve a simple puzzle or try to complete a more difficult one. She divided the children into two groups—those who chose the easy task and those who accepted the challenge. But why?

The distinction between the two groups of children had nothing to do with their abilities but with their underlying beliefs rather than their mindset. This is the underlying context for which I will consider two concepts that largely determine our development and success—fixed mindset and growth mindset.

FIXED MINDSET

People with fixed mindsets are those who think, consciously or unconsciously, that intelligence is unchangeable. Each of us is born with a certain degree of intelligence and a stable set of talents or qualities that are impossible to change. Based on this premise, they maintain a specific behavior:

- They tend to display good self-esteem to appear intelligent and skilled.
- They avoid challenges at all costs since failure would mean a lack of ability.
- They are defensive in the presence of an obstacle and quickly abandon tasks that pose a challenge.
- They are convinced that striving is futile and failing is unacceptable. They pursue infallibility.
- They feel threatened by both the success of others and criticism.

GROWTH MINDSET

On the other hand, those with a growth mindset believe they can develop skills and talent through hard work and commitment. They understand that each of us has initial baggage, but what matters is how we use it. They, therefore, exhibit the following behaviors and attitudes:

- They are eager to learn and grow.
- They accept challenges and use them as they see them as an opportunity for improvement.
- They see failure as part of the journey; they do not give up in the face of obstacles and persevere.

- They do not see effort as a lack of ability but rather as a path to excellence.
- They learn from constructive criticism and are inspired by the success of others.

The attitudes associated with the two different mindsets determine the development each of us can achieve. Those who belong to the first group (i.e., those who trust innate gifts) may grow quickly and then stall. On the contrary, people who belong to the second group (those who use more commitment and perseverance) continue to grow until they reach their full potential.

This would manifest itself in the educational field, their careers, social relationships, and any other area of life. Those with a growth mindset overcome obstacles, learn from mistakes, correct their shots, and grow and develop a better version of themselves.

The fixed mindset leads to stabilization once a certain level is reached—a story that will never be surpassed because of fear of failure. The paralysis one feels in the face of a challenge because of the limitation constituted by thinking that we are what we are, and that's it.

Although the type of mindset is part of the personality, it is within our power to change it. In what way? We stop esteeming ourselves or measuring our worth through innate qualities and begin to appreciate our commitment and ability to get back up and persevere. Sometimes failing allows us to reach our highest potential. Let's now take a look at the five areas to develop an action-taking mindset:

BUILD YOUR CIRCLE OF FIVE

The people we associate with and spend time with have elemental power over us—they can influence our values, behavior, and ambitions. We can say that what we accomplish in our lives, the goals we achieve, are in some way determined by the people around us, particularly the five people we spend most of our time with. It is a process of emulation that has belonged to us since childhood. Just as the child learns and replicates the behavior of adults, the adult tends to imitate other adults closest to them.

Sociology defines the people we associate with and who influence us as the peer group, which is decisive in creating our opinions and beliefs and directing our actions.

Therefore, while always remaining free to associate with whomever we wish, it is helpful to be aware of how much our relationships with those close to us contribute to determining our future. A person committed to achieving their own goals and constantly taking care of their personal growth can be "hindered" by the people they associate with, albeit in good faith and unconsciously.

An example may give you an idea: how hard will it be to stop smoking if you hang out with people who smoke and constantly offer you a cigarette? Here are three rules that mark our belonging to the group of reference against which it is essential to develop awareness:

1. We become similar to our peer group.

The dominant characteristics of the group we attend somehow become "contagious." If our peer group likes sports and is predominantly made up of sportsmen and women, we will likely become sportsmen and women; conversely, we will likely do the same if they frequent museums and art galleries.

2. To not differentiate ourselves from the people whose company we seek, we tend to meet our expectations.

Whether these expectations are positive or negative, it is rare for a person to exceed the expectations of their peer group.

3. If we hang out with people who have developed more of the skill we intend to pursue, we will elevate our standards.

If we hang out with a group that encourages the skill we want to develop, we will be better at that skill. Therefore, going along with the natural tendency to emulate, to accelerate our growth process, it is important to surround ourselves with people who have already reached a higher level in the areas we intend to improve on. Let's take an example. I want to get better at playing tennis. If I hang out with a group of good tennis players and train with them, I will undoubtedly get better at the game.

Have you ever questioned the type of people you spend the most time with? Does your target group represent an incentive for you to improve? Does it help you and support you in reaching your goals?

To help you clarify, I propose a simple exercise that will help you reflect on the influence of the people you usually hang out with on your life. Please take some time to think and write down the answers to these questions.

Think about the group you spend most of your time with and ask yourself:

- How do the people I hang out with influence me?
- How frequently do I ask them for advice?
- How important are their judgments?
- How do I behave when I have opinions and beliefs that differ from theirs?

- How do I use their thoughts and views?
- What do they expect of me?
- What kind of person do they want me to be?
- What would I be like if I was as precise as they wish?
- What perception would I have of myself if I was exactly as they wanted me to be?
- What perception would I have of myself if I looked like them?
- What aspects of their behavior would I want to act out?

After answering the questions above, I invite you to make a bulleted list of the various areas of your life (work, family, leisure, health, etc.) and identify all the people in the different regions who influence you. Now reread each name on the list and ask yourself these questions:

- How does this person help me achieve what I want?
- What kind of results have they achieved relative to what I desire?
- What kind of advice can I ask them for?
- Concerning my goal, where will their emulation take me?
- By gaining clarity on these issues, you will have a greater awareness of your peer group and its impact on you.

Where do these reflections take you? What awareness have you gained? Use this exercise to define the five truly enriching people you spend your free time with and limit your connections with toxic people. Before long, your results will automatically be different just by having this insight.

CONTROL YOUR SCHEDULE

If you want to make the most out of each week without stressing out and feeling rushed, this is the paragraph you've been subconsciously waiting to find. In the following few lines, you'll learn how to best plan and organize your week to complete all your commitments without forgetting to give yourself the attention you deserve.

It's Monday morning, the alarm clock goes off early, a new week is about to begin, and all you want is to experience the weekend again and stay in bed for as long as you want. You're overwhelmed with things to do, you always feel unable to complete them all, and you're perpetually living in a race against time that leaves no room for the items you want.

Suppose you recognize yourself even in a small part of that description. In that case, I want to reassure you because even if it seems complicated to believe, there is a way to reverse this situation entirely. By following the advice I'm about to give you, you'll be looking forward to Monday so you can start a new week full of enthusiasm, knowing precisely what to do and when to do it to accomplish your tasks quickly and without stress.

The magic begins by planning for your week. When we leave things to chance, the risk we run is that we forget our priorities, feel perpetually behind schedule, and feel like time is slipping away. If, on the other hand, we take a moment on Sunday to prepare for the week ahead by consciously deciding what direction to take our days, it will be much easier to get off on the right foot and be more productive and satisfied.

Planning allows you to simplify your life and make the most of your time consciously so that you can focus on the things that matter.

Define Your Weekly Goal

To start setting up your weekly schedule correctly, you'll need to define your goal. What do you want to get out of this new week? It could be taking a minor step toward your monthly goal or completing a commitment you've been putting off for a while. Whatever your weekly goal is, declare it by writing it down! It will be a daily reminder that you should focus all your efforts on completing it.

Write down your to-do list.

Every week, between work, home, family, and free time, there are many things to do. You often make the mistake of keeping everything in mind with the risk of forgetting important things and consuming your energy trying to remember what you have to do. Solving this problem is easier than you think; write a nice list of everything you have to do during the week to empty your mind. You will feel much lighter, will not forget anything, and will be aware of how many things you have done and how many are missing.

Schedule activities to do during the week

You can't complete a very long to-do list in a single day. The strategy to get things done is to narrow your list to only the top three priority tasks. Ignore the rest. Only work on what matters most. This will allow you to plan your high-level activities, optimize your work, and finish more in less time. For example, I can organize myself to grocery shop only once on a given day with a list already made to save time. Unlike what you might think, organizing and planning gives us much freedom.

One of the things that wastes the most precious time is

indecision… you know all the time you spend in front of your closet choosing what to wear or thinking about using the ingredients in your fridge to cook a balanced and tasty meal?

All those minutes added together is time that slips away without you even realizing it.

By determining in advance what to wear and eat over the week, you'll find yourself having extra free time you didn't think you had and feeling less stressed. You'll have one less thought and a more accessible mind to think about your true priorities.

Also, when planning your week, you are very focused on your duties and commitments; the risk you run is that you want to get as many things done as possible without considering your energy and needs. This is the wrong thing to focus on—It is impossible to be productive without dedicating time to ourselves. That's why you must include time every day to devote entirely to yourself in your weekly planning. The more you manage to carve out some time for yourself, the more your productivity will increase, and you'll be able to live your week to the fullest.

As you can see, with just a few steps and paying attention to the right things, you can create a weekly schedule that will simplify your life and allow you to stop dreading Monday. Make weekly planning an essential Sunday ritual, and you'll see that you can face even the most challenging days with new energy and awareness.

TRUST IN YOURSELF, YOUR MISSION

There are many reasons why so many adults feel sad, discouraged, have no confidence in the future, and are perpetually unhappy. But one of these reasons is spoken about very little, partly because it requires some general admission of guilt and partly because it's a sensitive subject, and in this fast-paced society, there's never time to go deep.

If so many feel inadequate, "out of place," confused, and unhappy, no one has taught them to believe in themselves. They haven't had the opportunity to learn the excellent incredible process of self-love, which is necessary to become adults capable of facing life with decisions and serenity.

You only have one life, and you don't want to live it playing a part. According to your own rules, you want to live it your way, realizing your true nature.

If you have to give up your nature to do so completely, you want to be someone other than the perfect partner, the perfect employee, or the ideal citizen. First, you should be the best version of yourself; that's the only "perfection" you aspire to. In this society of total homologation, being yourself means taking risks, and that's why so many people don't—they're afraid of failure.

But this is nothing more than a mental trap of your comfort zone, which is to believe that everything will be fine by following a particular path and obeying specific rules. You are bored and never fully happy in your comfort zone, but you don't risk anything.

Everything will always be fine inside that bubble. False. It's not like that at all. You can fail resoundingly even by making safe life decisions, even by falling perfectly within the concept of "normality," even when, in the eyes of everyone, you are behaving perfectly.

Everything can go wrong at any moment, even in your comfort zone. When you realize this, you understand that you have to believe in yourself and you have to do it strongly because if you run the risk of failing (and you always do), you have to do it while you are pursuing your dreams, while you are building your life path, created on the shape of your happiness. It's a tragedy to fail after thinking for years only and exclusively about being "right" for society and the people around you, and that is a total failure. On the other hand, if you fail while believing in yourself, it's a life lesson.

When you believe strongly in yourself, failure does not exist. You can achieve your dreams, or you can learn something new. Either way, you grow, evolve, and give your essence a chance to shine and express itself.

Try to imagine a lifetime of wearing the guise of just another person, so gray and anonymous that even they would have a hard time recognizing themselves among all the others. That prospect is frightening, and it's a wasted life.

Think about it once in a while. The fear of wasting your only chance will be the most vigorous push to start believing in yourself.

SET UP TRIGGERS IN YOUR ENVIRONMENT

Fact: The environment we live in influences our success index. Each of us has a space that inspires us and makes us feel alive. For example, some people love to live in the city because they are energized by it, while others feel overwhelmed in this environment. Some people are happy if they live near the sea, others prefer the mountains. Deciding where to live and work can significantly affect how you feel. And even if you can't afford to move right now, even the house you live in can become the environment that helps you stimulate your creativity.

Aided by the redesign of my studio, I've often thought about my surroundings. When I finished placing the last item in my completely renovated studio, I felt so happy and peaceful that I never wanted to leave. I spent Saturday night going in and out of my studio, looking at it before I went to sleep, maybe even dreaming about it.

I'm thankful that I completely changed my mind from my initial thoughts. And the pandemic, in this case, had a positive effect of keeping me from making an impulse buy and giving me time to think about my new studio and how I wanted it. Imagine, I had started buying all-black furniture, and now it's all bright and white instead!

It took me a very long time to achieve the result I can enjoy today. The search for my ideal space began when I was in high school. Over the years, I went from a shelf in the corner of the living room to a bedroom of my own, to a room connected to the house via the garage where, in the winter, I could start working only after I had turned on the heater for at least half an hour. And now I have my apartment with my brand-new studio. Each of these (more or less fortunate) spaces helped me realize how I wanted to handle it and allowed me to stimulate my creativity.

If you want to find a space like this without moving house, think about the environments that make you feel the way you want to experience. You can decide if you want to feel Energetic, happy, serene, or motivated. I suggest a journaling exercise, and in particular, I suggest you do a visual journal. Look through newspapers, vacation photos, or online for images or words describing your ideal environment.

Start by thinking about your outdoor environment—sea or mountain, desert or forest, countryside or city. If you choose the city, cut out photos of cities that inspire you and decide how the houses, stores, and streets should be. Start making a collage with these elements. Then look at it and check how you feel. If you want to feel energetic, and your collage makes you think that way, you're on the right track. If not, try again.

Now think about your living space and how you would like your home to feel. Again, I ask you to look for pictures and phrases. This time, you'll focus on colors and furnishings. Select the images and words and make another collage. Remember that you're not remodeling your house, so you can put anything you want in your visual journal, even if it's out of proportion, even if it's too expensive, and even if the people living with you wouldn't like it.

Now that you've let your imagination roam free look carefully at your collage and figure out what elements return and what patterns repeat. Choose five words that sum up most of the features that emerged from your observation. I did this exercise four years ago and completely forgot about it. And these days, I went to pick it up again. What were the five words I wrote down?

- Personal growth
- Books
- Energy
- Wealth
- Harmony & wellness (white)

There must be a reason I finally feel "at home" and inspired. And the same thing can happen to you, even if you don't have a room but just a desk in your living room or bedroom. Think about the five elements in your collage and try to reproduce them through colors, materials, and desk objects. Working in an environment that belongs to you will stimulate your creativity and help you achieve your goals, even those that seem more ambitious at the moment.

CONTINUE LEARNING

The world moves on, society, technologies, and everything around us evolves and transforms. We can't just stand by and watch because, otherwise, we would have missed something of this change, resulting in being left behind or, worse yet, excluded. The practical demonstration is that there is always something new to learn.

Everything evolves, including ourselves. Sometimes we get the feeling of "that something" we're missing, that skill that, once built, will make us feel more prepared. So, we try to understand what it is or what we want to be able to do, and once discovered, we decide to learn and enrich our lives. The term "training" indicates a process of developing the individual, leading to the progressive acquisition of specific professional skills through study and experience.

Training should be considered an element of transformation that allows individuals to acquire skills, competencies, and valuable aspects to determine a better insertion in the reality in which they operate.

The training objectives are linked, influenced, and associated with the project and the context in which it operates. What is certain is that, with training, it is possible to enrich skills, abilities, and behaviors that are now more than ever indispensable for any profession.

Today, with the job market still in crisis, what is emerging is that companies are demanding increasingly competent and specialized personnel. Giving value to one's skills through training for companies and people means investing in oneself and improving to achieve specific objectives.

Therefore, training can be an investment (which will become a gain) for both people and companies.

For some years, we have been discussing concepts such as "continuous training" and "lifelong learning," which means modifying or expanding the skills and knowledge to adapt them to the times. It is continuous learning in line with the changes in society. It is also a way to stay active, curious, and part of a "learning society." So, the adage is correct: "You never stop learning."

"Momentum is whatever your attitude determines it to be."

—Lou Holtz

8
CREATE A STRONG SENSE OF URGENCY

A lack of urgency is one of the primary reasons you are not achieving important goals. The willingness to take immediate action is the winning decision that puts you in the lead regarding getting fast results. Putting off something you could do now until later leads to a decline in motivation and desire.

How many times have you found yourself in need of resolving something? Often, have you found yourself needing to resolve a quarrel and preferred to put it off instead of taking action to fix it right away? You like to put it off indefinitely, and that small knot that could have been untied with a simple chat, over time, has turned into an inextricable tangle and is so big that it can only degenerate into quarrels or breakups. It would have been better to be far-sighted, resourceful, transparent beforehand, far-sighted, innovative, and acceptable ahead and move with a sense of urgency.

A leader always looks for resourceful people driven by a sense of urgency and accountability. This is because it is a mental habit of success that helps in everyday life, both personally and professionally. The moment you become aware of the importance of an action, you must execute and perform that action without hesitation.

Procrastination does nothing but create a mass of self-sabotaging thoughts in your mind, capable of clouding clarity, effectiveness, and efficiency. When you put something off, you're forced to live with a constant idea that reminds you that you have unfinished business. However, when you resolve that right away, your sense of self-worth, confidence, freedom, and inner lightness increases.

Remember to be moved by a sense of urgency—never put off until tomorrow what you can do today. This chapter will teach you eight ways to build speed into your action plan.

Custom-build your strategy to increase a sense of urgency based on personal goals.

Stopping procrastination would allow us to free ourselves from our anchors and head towards ambitious goals if we contextualize it in a larger project.

There are several techniques, such as the simple but effective "3-2-1" strategy; since we procrastinate on something, we start the countdown in our heads. When it ends, we commit to taking action without question.

Another simple technique is to make the first step necessary for the more significant action; for example, if we have to go for a run, the goal will be to tie our running shoes. If we have to start working on the computer, the plan will be to sit in front of it and turn it on. Break it down into a small and immediate step you can complete right away.

However, the best thing is to create your strategy and adapt it according to your needs and requirements. You can take inspiration from the two techniques I've just mentioned to make one tailored for you.

Make decisions with confidence and act quickly.

Becoming confident is undoubtedly not just a matter of putting on a few tricks. Some people advise you to take care of your posture, appearance, voice, or way of walking or talking, and these are all contrived remedies that serve little purpose.

You become a confident person when you can find the answers. It doesn't matter what others think. Now I'll show you a road map that I suggest you follow to develop confidence and deal with situations in which you are under the judgment of others and are called to make a choice.

- First, you need to develop healthy and authentic self-esteem. It will give you strength and make you immune to harmful and often unnecessary criticism.
- Then you need to learn how to manage your negative emotions to turn them into positive ones. These will always get you better results.
- I already mentioned mindfulness. The goal is to learn how to always find the answers you need, even in new situations.
- It would be best if you learned to overcome fear. This feeds anxiety and insecurities and becomes an obstacle to be removed immediately.

These are the steps I recommend you take now. Confidence doesn't come by magic. It is a process of awareness and personal growth that takes time and commitment. Quick action is implicit in the belief that you have made the right choice. Follow the little diagram I've given you, and you'll see your ability to take action take off.

Identify the potential obstacles and hack through them as you take action.

If your goal is to live the life you've always wanted, you must first understand that nothing (or almost nothing) happens by accident. If you don't define a clear strategy to hit your goals, if you don't commit yourself every day to achieve the results you've set for yourself, in the end, you risk ending up with nothing.

Now I want to ask you a fundamental question: do you think you are determined to achieve your goals? Have you defined them clearly? Have you thought of a concrete strategy that will allow you to acquire them?

But most importantly—and now we get into the heart of today's topic—do you feel ready to overcome the obstacles you will inevitably encounter? Think carefully about this fundamental point because you may have set clear goals and defined the right strategy to achieve them as long as you want. But, if you are not emotionally prepared to face the difficulties, everything will likely melt from one moment to the next, like snow in the sun.

Visualize taking action and the emotion you attach to achieving something.

This secret weapon, which is so valuable for achieving our goals, is none other than visualization. Our minds form a crystal-clear image of what we want to achieve. It is helpful to use pictures and visual reinforcements that help you remember your goal. A photograph, a drawing, a phrase, a famous quote, or a simple word—anything goes—as long as it helps you to bring to life this mental image, your vision of success.

An obvious example is that of athletes. Numerous studies in applied sports psychology have shown that visualization aids performance in sports. One of these studies found that just imagining lifting weights can bring about specific changes in muscle activity. Many top athletes use visualization to improve their performance and achieve specific goals. However, you don't have to be at their level to take advantage of visualization. Another study showed that even some novice golfers could improve their results by combining exercise with visualization instead of just exercising. Sports is just one example, but it does the trick in explaining what visualization is all about. Athletes train to improve and to win, right? What about you? What do you want to improve in your life? Do you want to "win" a degree, a job, a promotion, or a person?

Practicing visualization will help you achieve it. If you have a goal, here's how to get there:

- Practice visualization when you are relaxed. The best times for this exercise are the morning as soon as you wake up and the evening before you sleep.
- Be clear about what outcome you want to achieve and visualize it. Imagine what will happen when you accomplish that goal in detail. Think about how you feel, what you think, and your situation as if it were real. Because, in your imagination, it is accurate. Try to use your five senses when you imagine the scene to make it as realistic as possible.
- Be consistent in your practice of visualization. It will get easier with time and become your secret weapon to achieve the goals you set for yourself.

Visualization has great power because it creates images in our minds in which we see ourselves having everything we desire. This generates thoughts and emotions that make us feel like we have already achieved that goal in the present. In other words, think positively and imagine your life as you want it to be—only in this way will you have a chance to get what you want!

Identify your comfort zone activities and how to remove them during work times.

Everything that is known and familiar can be defined as a "comfort zone." This means that everyone has a "comfort zone." It is safe and protective because it is known.

Acting within the comfort zone feeds many of our illusions. For example, it deludes us about the controllability of the future, and it is a shield against the uncertainties of tomorrow. What could happen if you traveled the same commute to work every day?

The psychology behind these repetitive behaviors is well-known and understandable. Our brains act by taking shortcuts. Our very survival—even in a world as evolved as ours—is tied to ancestral mechanisms and stress responses. But is it essential to step out of your comfort zone? Why abandon a known environment in favor of an unknown one?

The answer is simple... because all performance, of whatever kind, tends to flatten out over time.

After a while, you tend to become complacent with your performance. And, if you think about it, this pattern of behavior is typical in many areas, not only in strictly professional ones. Many athletes arrive at the top of sports and then give up as soon as they have achieved sufficient earnings.

So, here's how to achieve change, break the chain of lousy habits, and glimpse a horizon beyond the usual path you take every morning. You must break out of your comfort zone to go towards something extraordinary. Try it every single day. Start changing in small steps. Your attitude towards new things will become more inclined, and your mind will be more resilient to the unexpected.

Read a book that's all about taking action.

Throughout this book, we have already observed how important it is to keep yourself knowledgeable and to learn. I will present the best motivational books ever written, capable of giving you an incredible charge to change your life, set great goals, and achieve them one after another.

Reading even just one of these motivational books could make all the difference in your life, transforming you into a more positive and better version of yourself. These are the top five books I recommend:

I. Think and Grow Rich - Napoleon Hill

Think and Grow Rich is one of the cornerstones of personal development and a must-read. It is a timeless classic in which the author has condensed his 20 years of research on wealth and success into a few brilliant principles.

It is a book that has inspired millions of people by transforming their lives and is so powerful that it can profoundly change how you perceive existence. It is the father of all motivational and personal growth books!

II. Unlimited Power - Anthony Robbins

Anthony Robbins is the number one coach globally; this is his most excellent classic and one of the best motivational books.

This book is a mandatory step for anyone planning a personal development journey. It opens your mind to the possibility of getting everything you want and feeling how you want—you completely control your life!

Tony's energy and passion, which are conveyed compellingly in this book, have been influential in giving direction to my whole life.

III. The Magic of Thinking Big - David Schwartz

The ability to think big separates extraordinarily successful people from mediocre people. David Schwartz challenges you, in the book, to choose grandiose goals and to pursue them with optimism by giving your all to achieve them.

What's more, The Magic of Thinking Big explains that intelligence, education, and knowledge do not always contribute to a person's success, but more so the ability to have a grand vision. If you want to get the most out of your life, you need to read this book!

IV. Drive - Daniel H. Pink

Drive is a book that we could define as disruptive in its intrinsic concept of motivation. For Daniel Pink, the old "carrot and stick" method not only doesn't work but sometimes can even be counterproductive. We often err in assigning a prize to our employees, friends, or family members' virtuous behaviors. And as a result, we also tend to punish them when they engage in destructive behavior.

The truth, according to Pink, is that people have an intrinsic motivation that drives them to do things well. People must be free to express themselves and direct their actions according to their aptitudes. This book is recommended for those with a strong entrepreneurial spirit and a solid creative disposition.

V. The Greatest Salesman in the World - Og Mandino

The Greatest Salesman in the World is a touching tale that uses the concept of sales as a metaphor for life to realize oneself and live a meaningful and prosperous existence.

This book by Og Mandino contains much food for thought and conveys values such as optimism, strength, awareness, genuine happiness, and love.

Imagine the outcome if you DON'T take action. Visualize where you will be and where you won't be

You can only feel motivated if you know what motivates you. If you want to improve the quality of your life, you must dig deep within yourself to understand why you want to put so much effort into your life to accomplish what is important to you.

If you often feel unmotivated, you need to know yourself better. To discover your deepest motivations, start with what you think is your most crucial current motivation for achieving your goal. For example, if your goal is to increase your income by 30% in the next six months, ask yourself the following questions:

- What might happen if I earn less?
- What are the disadvantages of staying at my current income level?

Then write down your answers and keep asking yourself questions until you find the strong motivation to get up every morning with plenty of energy and ready to pursue this goal.

Alternatively, you can imagine the outcome if you don't take action. Can you imagine yourself satisfied? I think not; this way, you will see what you don't want to achieve and commit to the opposite. Reaching the first goal is likely the beginning of a much larger life project.

Meditate to increase your energy mental energy.

Meditating is a beneficial practice that helps you relax your mind and ease anxiety and stress. But how do you do it? There are several techniques, but I propose the classic Zen exercise, and you'll find it easier than it sounds.

Have you ever really "meditated"? You may know more or less what it is, or it seems like an abstruse practice that doesn't fit in well with the meticulous organization of your days. You should meditate. All the more so if your life is hectic, full of un-cancellable commitments, things to do, people to see, events to attend, and errands to run.

The more structured your life is, the more risk you have of going haywire when things get out of control. I'm sure you know what I'm talking about. Do you ever wonder what you live for? Who are you? Do you ever listen to yourself in silence? Can you empty your mind and let the sensations from your body flow?

A good meditation doesn't take long, from a minimum of five minutes a day to a maximum of 15-20. As you can see, it's a matter of carving out just a little space in your busy day. Several techniques and exercises exist, but I propose a unique model with variations.

To understand how to do it, I have to explain what Zen meditation is. It's about focusing your attention on a unique "object" of interest, which can be honest and concrete or abstract. Let me give you an example. If you decide to pin your attention on the chair in front of you for five minutes of your time, you will analyze it in sequence:

- Its position, from bottom to top and from left to right
- Its origin (where you bought it from, for example)
- The material with which it is made
- The color and brightness according to the direction of the external light and how it hits it
- The shape, the geometry of the lines, and how they intersect each other

- The decomposition into individual parts
- Weight and volume
- What use you make of it, have made or could make of it
- Its past, present, and possible future (in the case of the chair, for example, the move to another environment, possible recycling with decoupage, or even the pulping)

The exercise should be repeated a second time with your eyes closed, keeping in mind the object in its mental dimension. The meditation ends when you can identify with the chosen thing.

A proper Zen meditation chases away those pesky, obsessive thoughts and gives you the appropriate detachment you need to face any life event, wanted or unexpected.

"Build confidence and momentum with each good decision you make from here on out and choose to be inspired."

—Joe Rogan

9
HOW TO PREVENT BURNOUT & NEVER GIVE UP

In truth, how many times have you said you feel unmotivated and lacking energy? Well, your condition is not isolated, but it shouldn't be taken lightly. If you've heard yourself say phrases like this, you might be one of a group of workers suffering from work-related stress to the point of suffering from burnout syndrome. Depersonalization and reduced capacity in the workplace, a form of exhaustion that is now considered almost a "normal" condition of modern work.

The phenomenon was first studied in the 70s in America and observed by the psychiatrist Maslach within the mental hygiene departments of the professionals who cared for patients. However, today, this malaise affects the so-called helping professions and is widespread and transversal. It affects women and men of all ages, belonging to the most diverse job profiles. But what are the causes of burnout? Is it possible to prevent it? If so, how? Let's find out together in this chapter. Happy reading!

CAUSES OF BURNOUT

Subjective

There are several psychological causes of burnout related to emotional stress. This burnout can directly impact people dealing with other people's problems in their jobs—nurses, police officers, tax collectors, lawyers, or service industry workers. In most cases, this stress arises from the emotional involvement that comes with the nature of the relationship.

When, due to character, type of work, or lack of self-knowledge, you cannot manage empathy and fully detach, there is an identification with the problems of others that causes an excessive stress load. In this case, burnout represents natural wear and tear on those who suffer it, who feel drained of their energy.

Objectives

There are, however, new causes that generate burnout. Today, the phenomenon is attributable to the characteristics of the current world of work and modern lifestyles. Performance anxiety is a typical phenomenon in our society, involving even school-age children.

Young people, in particular, often come up against a working environment that is not what they want or are suited to, with dynamics and working conditions that sacrifice the human side in favor of purely economic logic. This can generate intense stress. Often, one realizes this late, and it sometimes leads to sudden and non-rational decisions, such as self-dismissal, absenteeism, or behavioral disorders that cause the person's removal by his superiors.

Objective causes of burnout, brought about by working conditions and dynamics, include:

- Poor pay
- Overtime (poorly paid or free)
- Lack of protection and incentives
- Stressful external environment (as is the case, for example, with constant lighting and music in many retail stores)
- Competition

- Incommunicability between departments and roles
- Insufficient gratification
- Mobbing dynamics (psychological persecution).

Moreover, for a thorough analysis of the objective causes of burnout, we must remember that today the ability to work under stress is one of the requirements often asked in job interviews.

This, in addition to the organizational nature of companies that are often only profit-oriented, now requires a solid commitment to the person, time, and energy, even at the expense of private life and, usually, in exchange for little or no gratification. When you can no longer manage all this stress, you experience a sort of short-circuit, exhaustion, which manifests with some typical symptoms of burnout syndrome. Let's see together what they are.

HOW TO RECOGNIZE IT

The symptoms of this malaise are related to anxiety, depression, and behavioral disorders. When we are victims of work-related stress, we tend to feel very tired and unable to recover energy, even during the weekend. In addition, our thoughts are always negatively turned to work, which we try in every way to avoid. In particular, burnout syndrome can manifest itself through:

- High resistance to going to work every day
- Feeling of failure
- Anger and resentment
- Sense of guilt and disesteem
- Discouragement, indifference, cynicism
- Isolation
- Feeling tired all day
- Difficulty in concentrating

- Problems with insomnia
- Addictive diseases of all kinds (alcohol, drugs, gambling, food mania)
- Headaches and gastrointestinal disorders
- Conflicts with colleagues, spouses, and family members
- High absenteeism

In addition to these common symptoms, there are three characteristic phases of burnout phenomenology.

Three Phases

- A feeling of helplessness characterizes emotional and nervous exhaustion. One feels drained from work.
- In response to the malaise, the individual initially tends to adopt cynical, detached, or aggressive attitudes at work and toward the problems of others.
- Chronic depression or apathy. One feels inadequate and incapable and develops negative and resentful thoughts about oneself.

Dr. Beverly Potter, a social and group psychology specialist, has created a short test to recognize burnout syndrome. By answering a few simple questions, you will get a score indicating whether you are subject to this malaise.

Addressing and improving this stress condition is essential to becoming aware of this state and then undertaking a path of help.

HOW TO PREVENT BURNOUT

It would help if you addressed Burnout Syndrome as soon as possible. At the same time, it is also essential in our days to recognize emotions that hinder us in relationships or create conflicts that bring stress.

In addition, if we feel overwhelmed by anxiety and tension, we must try to communicate this with people near and dear to us. If all this is difficult, it is appropriate to seek support from a professional psychologist, who can help and support you on a path to regaining well-being. In addition, if you are an entrepreneur, it is essential to learn those techniques that allow you to control or eliminate work-related stress. To prevent burnout syndrome, you need to:

- Get enough sleep to recover and have enough energy during the day.
- Have a balanced lifestyle concerning pace, nutrition, training, and time for yourself.
- Exercise regularly.
- Define priorities and boundaries to focus resources and energies on the activities that bring us the most feedback.
- Control the time spent on emails and smartphones, giving yourself a clear and precise rule to respect at certain times of the day.
- Establish clear limits concerning working hours, which are the boundaries of your well-being and your private life.
- Have a quality social life, unplug, and share to avoid feeling overwhelmed.
- Read and be informed (books to manage, combat, and overcome stress).
- Organize your work well to prevent loss and waste of time, unexpected events, disorganization, and harmful stress.
- Delegate.
- Learn to say no.

- Work for well-defined objectives and detailed action plans to increase the probability of obtaining results.
- Have free time, cultivate hobbies outside work to dissociate from work, relieve accumulated stress, and reconcile work and family.
- Work to reduce travel and conduct business in a quiet, more accommodating space.

After looking at the list, think about your days… how many of these are things you already do? If you want to put these tips into practice, remember that you have to start with a mindset focused on your well-being, then try to change as you go along.

When we realize that work dynamics are invading our private lives, it is good to act promptly and ask for outside help without any shame or fear of being "wrong." This is particularly important for men, who are likelier to ignore the problem and want to prove they can handle it, according to the stereotype of "the man who must never ask."

The path to help is based on changing and analyzing our reaction and communication mechanisms and learning how to manage and improve them. While it is true that we cannot change the work system and its dynamics, we can work on ourselves and scale back on our expectations. This does not mean settling, but instead not overloading the emotional investment we make in our work. It also means understanding whether or not we are doing the job we are suited for, and if not, considering a change of role or department rather than asking to be fired or continuing to work badly under stress.

Knowing one's limits, adjusting one's expectations to reality, and implementing relational strategies to improve communication and manage stress are all skills that help the individual on this journey. Burnout syndrome is an increasingly relevant phenomenon in the Western world. If society were to invest more in psychological prevention, including implementing guidelines to combat work-related stress, already widely discussed by the scientific community, there would be a collective benefit in health and work performance.

SHORT TEST ON BURNOUT

Read one sentence at a time and write down the number corresponding to your answer. In the end, add up the scores for each sentence. You can write your answers in a notebook or journal.

Instructions: 1 = rarely; 2 = sometimes; 3 = wouldn't know; 4 = often; 5 = all the time:

I feel tired even after a good night's sleep ____
I am dissatisfied with my work ____
I get sad for no apparent reason ____
I am forgetful ____
I am irritable and abrupt ____
I avoid others at work and in my private life ____
I sleep with difficulty (because of work worries) ____
I get sick more than usual ____
My attitude toward work is "Who cares"? ____
I come into conflict with others ____
My work performance is below par ____
I drink or take medication to feel better ____
Communicating with others is a struggle ____
I can't concentrate on work like I used to ____
Work bores me ____
I work hard but produce little ____

I get frustrated at work ____
I go to work unwillingly ____
Social activities exhaust me ____
Sex is not worth it ____
When I am not working, I watch TV ____
I don't expect much from work ____
I think about work during my free time ____
My feelings about work interfere with my private life ____
My work seems useless/purposeless ____

SCORE
25 to 50 - Everything is OK
51 to 75 - Better take some preventive measures
76 to 100 - You are a candidate for burnout
101 to 125 - Ask your family doctor for help

"Forward momentum only worked as a strategy if one had correctly identified which way was forward."

—Lois McMaster Bujold

CONCLUSION: TAKE THE FIVE-DAY MASSIVE ACTION CHALLENGE

Without a massive action plan, even the most inspiring goal can fall short. Below, we'll look at a five-day challenge to set a highly effective action plan for taking massive action and achieving our results in a far more streamlined approach. So, arm yourself with a pen and paper, and let's get started.

In one of the book's previous chapters, we saw how to create a well-formed goal. Now I invite you to choose a plan you want to accomplish within the following year.

DAY 1: THE GOAL

Dedicate the first day to writing a few lines explaining why it is a "must" for you to achieve.

- What are the reasons why you will achieve this goal at all costs?
- Why do you want to achieve it?
- Why is it important to you?

I invite you to proceed with reading and following the exercises of this challenge only after you have completed this step. This short first exercise will give you a way to understand your motivation and the purpose for which you want to achieve your goal.

Knowing what you want to achieve is essential, but more is needed to motivate you entirely or to make you go beyond limits, difficulties, and pain. The real reason for acting on your beliefs lies in the purpose. That can be, for example, the joy of personal achievement, pride, security, satisfaction in confirming your value, self-esteem…

Think about it… everything you do is not for money, fame, or power. The real reason is that you want to feel certain emotions. You want to feel important, safe, and happy. We go to great lengths for the emotions our goal would give us!

DAY 2: VISUALIZE YOUR SUCCESS

On the second day, we will imagine our goal as already achieved. Don't skip this step—it's essential. Take your time and truly visualize your success. The purpose of the second day is to create an anchor in our mind, a positive reinforcement that will keep us on the road through difficult times.

Numerous scientific studies show not only that it works but also how and why it works. From a scientific perspective, researchers have found that visualization works because the neurons in our brains interpret images the same way they interpret real-life activities.

In other words, when we visualize an action we want to perform or a result we want to achieve, we can "trick" our brains into believing we've already completed that action or achieved that goal. Okay, but how can we apply visualization to real life? And how can it be used to achieve a goal? I want to share with you three valuable strategies that I use for visualization myself:

I. The Mind's Gym

Close your eyes and imagine walking along a path surrounded by nature. Now imagine that you reach an open door, cross it, and climb the steps that lead to a sacred place accessible only to you.

On your path, you will be accompanied by two authoritative people for whom you have esteem and respect. They will be two mentors you choose who will have advice and suggestions to give you about the goal you want to achieve. Watch yourself realize a vital life goal with their advice.

II. The Deep Pond

Please close your eyes and imagine walking beside a stream flowing through the woods, its frothy course interrupted by rocks and fallen branches. These interruptions represent your "busy" mind. You sense the breeze blowing through the trees, the sun glinting through the leaves, the clear sky, and the animals in harmony with their surroundings and with you. The stream's flow finally widens into a pond with calm, clear waters.

You feel compelled to dive in and swim until you find an inviting and comfortable resting spot submerged in the clear water at the bottom of the pond. In this special, cozy, quiet place where you can feel protected, you sense how all feelings of fear are washed away by the purifying action of the water.

This stillness represents the deepest part of your soul. With gratitude, surrender and allow yourself to float to the surface. Feeling rejuvenated, resume your journey along the path from which you came.

III. Future Me

This visualization will help you learn how to plan your path to achieve a significant life goal mentally.

It could be losing 40 pounds, winning a significant sports competition, passing a challenging exam, or getting promoted.

See yourself as a vibrant person full of energy that illuminates your efforts.

You are physically strong, mentally alert, influential, respected, energetic, present, beautiful, well-grounded, and centered. The sun is shining, and the sky is clear. You note the date and time, and everything seems perfect. You knew this day was coming. Acknowledge and appreciate all your work; it's the decisive action you need to turn your dream into reality.

You realize your goal by creating it in your mind, step by step. Feel the gratitude and express it to those who have supported you on the journey—loved ones, friends, family, and colleagues. Smile and hug them. This achievement was the work of many people whose flags you carry.

Day 3: Structure Your Action Plan

After working on your goal and clarifying your purpose, brainstorm everything you need to do to achieve it. Space it out, be creative and detailed, and include even the simplest things. Help yourself with these questions:

- What do I need to do? What are the actions required to accomplish my goal?
- Where will I do it? In what context will I take those actions?
- How am I going to do it? Which are the ways I will perform the required steps?
- Give a date for each action you need to take: When does this need to be done?
- Who will do these actions? Are there tasks you can delegate, or will you do everything yourself?

Put these individual actions on your timeline, i.e., your calendar—whether it's a diary or the calendar on your phone, and ensure that each deadline is strictly pinned down.

Great, your plan is ready! Our goals can only be achieved through good planning that we must believe in and act upon.

DAY 4: THE ACTION CROSSROAD

I'll leave you with another tool I often use so that you have caught everything and can clearly understand your actions. Take another sheet of paper and draw a cross that takes up all the space, creating four quadrants.

I. In the upper left quadrant, write 'Resources', then list all the help you have available—time, money, tools, training, people (coach, athletic trainer, mental coach, family, a teacher, nutritionist...), books, inner resources such as determination, certainty, flexibility.

II. In the top right quadrant, write 'What I need to/can start doing'; here, list all those actions and behaviors you need to start doing to reach your goal.

III. Write 'What I need/can continue to do' in the third quadrant. Here, list all the actions and behaviors you already do that work and are committed to maintaining.

IV. Write down 'What I must/can stop doing' in the fourth quadrant. Here, list those dysfunctional and unhelpful behaviors/attitudes that have kept you from your goal until now.

Now you have everything you need to be super effective! All you have to do is continue with the last step, and you will have created a blueprint for your goal. On your part, it will take commitment, consistency, and resilience. Thanks to this road map, you've taken all the creative work off your shoulders, and you have to go along with it day after day.

DAY 5: HONOR YOUR INTENTION

Today, keeping promises and honoring commitments have become weak and improvised values, whereas once upon a time, a person's word was as valuable as their signature. People thought carefully about their ability to keep promises before agreeing to anything; it was indeed a more respectful way to live!

When you commit, you must ensure it's a good deal for yourself. Not keeping focused on the goal is somehow betraying yourself, which causes you to lose self-esteem. You lose confidence in fulfilling your commitments, weakening your sense of integrity. In short, not doing what you say you're going to do creates confusion, doubt, and uncertainty. Believe me when I tell you that it's just not worth it!

One helpful way to fulfill your commitment is to make a statement to yourself. Another way is to establish a consequence if you do not stick to your commitment. Push yourself forward by setting a price if you fail to keep a promise. The important thing is that you perceive the price you pay so high that you will have to stick to your commitments, whatever it takes.

The consequence, in short, should consist of something you want to avoid, such as paying a certain amount of money to a person or an organization that you do not like or shaving your hair off.

If you want to achieve a goal, you must commit to keeping your promises to yourself. This will make you valuable. Remember that you are only as good as your word; therefore, never break it.

—Scott Allan

"With momentum, you can literally do anything. Momentum is the energy that takes a few small steps and turns the results into something you could never see coming."

—Tim Denning